NATURAL BORN FIGHTERS

For Dad.

There comes a time when most sons realise that their fathers are not superheroes. For me it was the other way around. I started out by thinking that mine was nothing special but soon discovered that he was a true hero. His fierce temper and immense fighting skill were reserved for the street, away from our eyes. His wisdom came from no formal education and his complete devotion to us — his family — I am striving to copy.

MAINSTREAM / SPORT.

NATURAL BORN FIGHTERS

THE REAL FIGHT CLUB

CRAIG GOLDMAN

MAINSTREAM
PUBLISHING
EDINBURGH AND LONDON

This edition 2004

Copyright © Craig Goldman, 2002
All rights reserved
The moral right of the author has been asserted

First published in Great Britain in 2002 by
MAINSTREAM PUBLISHING COMPANY (EDINBURGH) LTD
7 Albany Street
Edinburgh EH1 3UG

ISBN 1 84018 836 7

A catalogue record for this book is available from the British Library

Typeset in Berkeley and Hammer
Printed and bound in Great Britain by
Cox & Wyman Ltd

ONE

ALAN MORTLOCK, THE MAN BEHIND THE UNDERGROUND WORLD
of unlicensed boxing arrived at Jefferson's Bar and Grill in
Buckhurst Hill, Essex, late for our meeting.

He bowled through the double doors, with fight tapes and rolled
up fight posters under his arm. His rolling walk, barrel chest and
stocky, muscular arms that stretched his black leather jacket, gave out
the unmistakable message: don't mess! His shaven head, immovable,
on top of the solid neck, set on square shoulders, gave him a stone-
hard look, and a relaxed, open stance that shouted confidence and
purpose. It said, 'This is me – I'm hiding nothing, I fear nothing, take
me as you find me or not at all.' He scanned the four people standing
at the bar and picked me out. He looked me over, snarled as if
disgusted by what he saw and came over.

'Alan? I'm Craig.'

'Oh yeah,' he said, 'I thought so.'

Seeing me had confirmed all that he expected. A flabby,
overweight, middle-class man in designer glasses, who probably
wanted to do another 'ban unlicensed boxing' TV programme: a stitch
up. I didn't know it then but the real reason he turned up was to
check me out and try and convert me into an unlicensed fight
believer. I opened the conversation by telling him about my plans for
a documentary to find out if unlicensed boxing still existed. ('Oh

yeah,' he confirmed.) And if it did, what it was like for the fighters.

'Go on,' he said.

I told him that Channel 5 had commissioned me to make a documentary about unlicensed boxing, bare-knuckle fighting and something called 'no-holds-barred wrestling'.

'Unlicensed boxing has nothing to do with bare-knuckle fighting or no-holds-barred,' he said.

Obviously not, I told him, fearing I'd lost him. I'd keep them separate and make sure we showed the differences. We began to talk about Alan Mortlock's world of unlicensed boxing.

He began by telling me about the way he saw his unlicensed boxing events. His fighting was an alternative to the normal boxing seen on the television, he said. It follows the same rules as boxing but the fighters are not training every day; they do other things for a living and the fights are just that – fights; more exciting and more aggressive than any that you might see in licensed professional boxing.

I didn't have a clue what he was talking about: how could a boxing match be different from a 'fight'? Over the next few weeks I would find out exactly what a big difference there was.

We moved from the bar to a quiet corner table away from prying eyes and ears and ordered some food. Soon the table was covered with plates of potato skins, onion rings, garlic dips, sheets of glossy A3 paper and a bottle of Chardonnay. Drink, food and fighting – who could ask for anything more?

It didn't take long to find out why Alan had chosen to meet at Jefferson's. During the conversation a stream of people kept interrupting, some coming up to the table, shaking Alan's hand and paying their respects. When they'd left our table to join their friends at the bar, Alan leant forward and whispered with a nod in their direction.

'They're friends of mine, serious people. It's not for me to judge them, mind.'

He returned to the subject of unlicensed boxing. He slipped the elastic bands off the roll of half a dozen posters and began to spread them out. It was unbelievable – here was the whole world of unlicensed boxing laid out on the table before me. The posters advertised recent unlicensed events, with photographs of fighters, their names and the area they came from printed underneath. Hard-looking men from Essex and east London; Ricky Judd from Basildon; African Charley from Walthamstow; Mark Patrick from Ilford; Liam McCarthy from Edmonton; and someone called 'Mud Morgy' from Romford. Sponsors' names and addresses crammed the bottom third of the posters – small companies, local businesses whose owners enjoyed the association with the unlicensed game and the VIP treatment they got on the night of the event. Terry's Tattoos, Scotty's Tyres, Thames' Bookmakers and Emporium Jewellers of Wickford.

Each poster told me that Alan's unlicensed world was alive and well and living in Essex. It is hidden from most of us who don't know where to look for it or who to ask about it. These guys don't have a newsletter that tells you about the next unlicensed event, they don't have a friendly website that advertises forthcoming attractions. You can't look them up in the Yellow Pages under BOXING, UNLICENSED. You wouldn't see the posters, because they are displayed in places and areas of London that you probably wouldn't go to: snooker halls, boxing gyms, bookmakers, tattoo shops, car mechanic workshops, pubs and private clubs. In Alan's words, his world was a closed shop. The people in it made arrangements by word of mouth; only a small group of people knew when and where the next fights were happening. Despite the posters, most of the people find out about Alan's events from the fighters or the fighters' family and friends. In pubs and clubs around east London, and sometimes south London, close friends tell their friends and so it goes on. It's done quietly – no fuss or frills, almost in secret, out of the corners of mouths in lowered voices. It's handled more like a dodgy business transaction than a sporting event. It's this illicit feel that's part of its appeal.

If I doubted the existence of unlicensed boxing half an hour before meeting Alan, I didn't now. Here in front of me I saw that it did indeed exist, and that it was well organised.

Here, on these posters that openly advertised the fights that were supposed to be underground events, the whole world of unlicensed boxing seemed somehow to be open, non-threatening. As more posters were unfolded, more fighters glared out and their names leapt off the page. THE BERMONDSY BANGER. SUGAR SHANE STANTON. SCRAP IRON MIKE. From the photographs on the poster you could tell that these men were not highly tuned athletes. Hard street fighters and pub brawlers yes, but highly trained boxers? No. They had something of the *look* of boxers, they posed like them with their bandaged hands raised high to protect their heads, their bodies pushed forward in the classic boxing pose, ready to defend or attack. But you could also see they were fighters, not technicians. The real thing. 'Propa.'

One poster stood out from the rest. It had a bright yellow background with the words Ultimate Fighting & Boxing in big, bold, red letters printed right across the top third. Underneath, it said: Last Man Standing, and below, the date of the event – Sunday, 20 February 2000 at The Epping Forest Country Club, Abridge Road, Chigwell, Essex.

This poster stood out not only because it was advertising something called 'Ultimate Fighting', but because it promoted an event happening only three weeks away at a place not four miles from where we were sitting. Alan had been organising it for the past two months and as he explained what it would be like I began to see that his world was indeed like an exclusive club.

'Characters!' he said. 'That's what we've got in this game, characters. Someone asked the Battersea Banger how he thought he was gonna get on with his fight and he said the other fella was gonna wake up with a crowd looking down at 'im. You got characters in the game. We work hard but it's a laugh.'

Smiling now, more relaxed, Alan was talking louder, making great sweeps with his hands. With a gleam in his eye he was talking about fighters like they were his naughty children.

'Chrissy Morris – one of my fighters – the Martini Kid. I've been in the corner with him, trying to tell him what to do and he's telling me jokes. People say that that's not on, but, he's a fantastic fighter: 60, 70, 80 bouts with only a few losses. A character and a fighter. The Martini Kid: any time, any place, anywhere. They're all good friends, my fighters. They all join together on the night and we're friends.'

'If they're not training all the time, what sort of jobs do they have?' I asked. Alan was guarded – he didn't want to give any information away about anyone. As we had only just met and he didn't know me, I couldn't blame him. Or perhaps he just didn't know.

He continues: 'These men can all hold their hands up and have a row but that doesn't mean they know how to box. You take a man into the gym and you work with that man for three or four months, get to know him, become friends with him, and you see his ability getting sharper as the weeks progress. In the build-up to the fight, the talk starts, the general chit-chat about it, and what's going on in the scene, 'cos it's not just about that night, it's about who's doing what and what's happening and who's won what. There's a social side to it, seeing people, having a laugh, having a joke. I think it's great. The other week I walked into the Peacock Gym in Canning Town – a fantastic gym down there. We was waiting in the foyer where you have your cup of tea and I was a bit early. All of a sudden the door opened and all the boys came in and it was: "Hey! How are you going?" and "You know what we are doing tonight?"

'Even putting your kit bag in the car and going up the gym, or taking them on the pads and then finally seeing that man get in the ring . . . everything comes together on the night. I don't spend time with them for nothing, I don't get no money out of them. I want to see 'em win. I'm over at Wanstead Park with Paul Kavanagh, watching him run up hills with logs on his back. And I'm saying to Paul, when he wants to stop – "Is the other man you're fighting running up hills with logs on his back Paul?" Whatever form of training we're doing, whether I'm pushing him through, or taking him swimming, or doing all sorts of different things to bring that boy on – it all comes out on the night. And then when you see that boy win – which my Paul did – then it's all worth it.'

Alan was then, and still is, 100 per cent sincere, speaking honestly, openly and bluntly. What he said he meant. And you believed it, because of the way he said it, no doubts or hesitation, clear and concise. If he didn't want to tell you something he would say he didn't know and leave it at that. He loved the unlicensed game and the fighters in it. For him nothing about it was wrong or dishonest or barbaric, it was something that would – and should – go on if he had anything to do with it.

'And then afterwards, win, lose or draw, everybody's happy, you know?' he continues. 'All right, there's losses, people don't win all the time, but if you get there with your fighter, and you've put everything into that boy then that's all you can do. He's gotta do the fighting; all I can do is guide him up to it. I don't get in there on the night with the kid – but someone like Paul Kavanagh, he can go a long way. When that man gets in that ring, it's just him and his opponent. It's a case of "May the best man win". And if you go away and you've had a result on the night, there ain't no better feeling. Even if you've gone away and lost, I've always said that there's no shame in losing 'cos any man who steps through them ropes to me is a hero. It's as simple as that.'

In the weeks and months that Alan prepared for the Last Man Standing show he had many things to do. Each aspect presented its own problems – the fighters being the main one.

Every fighter's greatest fear is losing his fight badly, not giving a good show, looking like a mug, someone who cannot fight. Every fighter on Alan's bill will have his supporters there on the night: family, friends, their girlfriends. It's more than the embarrassment, it's the fighter's reputation that's at stake. He sticks his chin out in the ring and invites his opponent to take his best shot. But he also presents himself to be judged by the people outside the ring and they can be harsh. They judge instantly and ruthlessly – sometimes with humour ('If they carry on like that there'll be a fight in a minute!'), sometimes with venom ("it 'im you wanker!'), and sometimes in cockney rhyming slang ("it 'im on the gunga din!' [hit him on the chin]).

Alan's fighters look to him for comfort and confidence building and before a fight his mobile phone is constantly busy. Fighters want to know that the man they are fighting is good and won't make the fight look like a walkover – but at the same time not too good so that the fighter will be beaten badly. They want tips about training, fighting and about life. They come to Alan with their personal problems. They tell him about the insults they have endured, money that is owed to them, that has not been paid, and respect not shown. Mostly Alan just listens. He does not judge them, just offers fitness and pre-fight preparation tips, reassures them and takes the next call.

While the fighters are phoning with their concerns, Alan designs the posters, hires the ring, organises the boxing gloves, keeps the Epping Forest Country Club happy, books the doctor and the paramedics, keeps the sponsors happy, arranges security, and he makes arrangements for and with the various managers and promoters. The sponsors – friendly shopkeepers, gym owners, car showroom owners and builders' merchants – all play their part. Alan trains his small band of select fighters at two gyms: the Peacock Gym and the Epping Forest Country Club members' gym.

Like most people I had no idea what the atmosphere of an unlicensed fight would be like. 'It's like a family affair,' Alan says. 'Some boys might have fought each other two or three times. It's a buzz, an adrenaline rush. Different gyms will fight each other locally, they come together on the night and the fans come and you've gotta be there to see how it generates excitement in everybody. It's a passion. It's our sport.'

Alan's enthusiasm, his total commitment, was infectious. Getting caught up in the brotherhood of it all was easy. I wanted to know more about the Last Man Standing event that was coming up in three weeks. Alan slipped easily into promoter mode.

'What people are gonna actually see on the night is boxing, ultimate combat (which is classed as Vale Tudo – literally translated: "anything goes" – which is a sport in itself) and kick boxing. So they'll actually see three fighting sports on the day.'

It was going to be an evening of fights between men from two gyms: the East London Champions Gym in Walthamstow and the Averly Gym that lies in the shadow of the Dartford Bridge, heading eastwards. A head-and-shoulders shot of two fighters facing each other filled half the poster. Underneath one fighter were the words The Best from the West – The One And Only 'Sugar S' from the Averly Gym. The other was billed as The Beast from the East – Vale the Russian. They would be fighting for something called the Ultimate Fighting Championship Title in three five-minute rounds. I still had no real idea what ultimate fighting was but I made a mental note to find out. Was it legal, for instance?

'It's legal but it's just not licensed by the Boxing Board of Control,' says Alan. 'It's licensed by the local council. I'd like to invite anybody along, from the Board, or from the British Medical Association – whoever – to see how strictly all the promoters that are using the event on the day run their shows. We are open for people to come along and see. I mean the promoter that we'll be using this time is a very professional guy – strict: two doctors, ambulances, everything will be there. It will be a very, very exciting day.'

Alan's unlicensed events follow the Queensbury rules and are not illegal. They have rounds, a referee, boxing gloves, gumshields and doctors at the ringside. If you wanted to take part in one of these events you could and they couldn't touch you for it. But of course you have to be a special type of person to want to join in.

'I think that the guys who take part in all this, whether they've had a street fight or a fight in the playground as a kid, they've gone on to fight in the ring or on the mats. Whatever way you want, fighting's fighting. I believe it's in us; it's in us all – and if we can't do it ourselves, then we like to watch people who can. You can go right the way back, even before the days of Rome. Boxing originated in Greece and it was called pancratium. Men would fight with the "fistus", their hands would be wrapped in leather, sometimes with metal studs embedded; other times they would roll their fists, band with straps, in glue made from the sap of trees and then rub them into shattered glass – imagine getting hit with that. It went from that to "iron glove", and then from that back to bare knuckle and all the way through to the modern boxing glove.

'I think men wanna prove themselves, prove that inside there is always that person who wants to get out, to be a fighter. It's been there since time immemorial hasn't it, that people wanna fight? And people wanna watch, and maybe the people that come and watch wanna be in there fighting but don't wanna get in there and *do* it, don't wanna do the training. I mean if you look at all the fighting sports that are drawing big crowds – people do wanna see it. And it's been with us for thousands of years. And it's never gonna change.

'You're just gonna see different fighting sports coming. As long as they're safe and they're regulated and the fighters are looked after, then there's nothing to worry about.'

When bare knuckle was mentioned Alan became uncomfortable. He didn't want to be associated with it. But he couldn't escape the fact that when people think of unlicensed fighting bare knuckle is what they imagine. As far as Alan was concerned, bare knuckle was a million miles away from his sport.

'I wouldn't wanna know about it, wouldn't wanna see it – not interested in it whatsoever. I think it's bad news really. Again, it's up to the guys: if they wanna do what they wanna do then, it's not for me to turn round and say that they shouldn't. But personally it doesn't do anything for me, you know? People are gonna get severely hurt – you know, smashing their knuckles, smashing their faces, cuts here there and everywhere. That's the reason that boxing gloves were brought in really.

'But then professional boxing originated from bare-knuckle fighting. You know? That was the origin of the red corner or the blue corner. This was where they used to tie the ribbons from around their waists. When they came in to fight, they use to peg their area, by taking off their ribbons and putting them on their corner.

'We use people at our shows to get the fighters out called "whips". If you read the history of boxing, whips were there to keep the crowd away in the early 1800s. They used to whip the crowd away, so they didn't get stuck into the fighters, or each other, and stop the action. That's where the term whips originated.

'So it was out of that that pro boxing came about. It's not that far from bare-knuckle boxing. But with better training, medical support and gloves. Really it's not that far away from the original.

'As far as unlicensed boxing goes, *our* fighting – in the old days "unlicensed" was not like boxing, it was more of a street-fight in the ring – people biting, head-butting and kicking while others were on the floor. The fights were held in breakers' yards or empty forgotten warehouses, using oil drums to mark out the ring. But it's not like that now. We've moved forward; it's the new millennium. This is what we're doing. We have given a say to the people who don't wanna box amateur and can't box pro – not because of their ability, because if they had the time to train, with their ability they would be at the top of the professional boxing world.

'Our boxing is for the businessman and the stockbroker and the builder. And the guy that wants to get in there and do it and go home and be proud of himself, his family patting him on the back and his kids shouting, "Yeah, go on dad!" That's what our sport's about.'

So Alan's sport is somewhere between professional boxing and amateur boxing, it allows men who want to fight with the Queensbury rules to do so in relative safety, in front of their family and friends. It isn't illegal, it just isn't licensed by the British Boxing Board of Control.

He sees the future of his sport very clearly. His is boxing that is outside the corruption and strict restraints of the professional fights that you see televised. His is a more down-to-earth version, open to everyone who wants to train properly and play by the rules – another way of proving oneself in the 'virtual' age of the internet and video games.

Alan says: 'I'm a founder of the World Prize Ring Association, which brings together groups of promoters. Instead of being splintered around and doing their own thing, I bring them together under the association. We work with six or seven of them now, to promote their own individual shows, at the Epping Forest Country Club, under one banner, the World Prize Ring Association.

'We have our own championship fights, with line-ups from the south of England, Britain, the Commonwealth, inter-continental, right up to world line-ups. That is my job, if you like. We're now issuing our own World Prize Ring Association licences to our own fighters. In the last 12 months we were really getting it laid down, moving forward.

'We've got certain people that are now coming in as backers, who see plenty of mileage in what we are doing, and who have got a love for the sport. One guy in particular is Ian Wilson, a businessman. He used to be a fighter. He's one of the main sponsors of these events. He wants to see it regulated and he wants to see the fights licensed. He's thrown his lot in behind us. There's good people now that really wanna see this move forward.'

Fighting was in Alan's blood, he loved every bit of it. 'Dad boxed,' he says. 'My Uncle Dick was a boxer. And he was a street fighter. He had plenty of bouts in the East End. So, yeah, and it's always been in the background, fighting. It's coming through me to my sons whether it be in the ring, or on the mats, or on the pavement or whatever. I'm not glorifying that but my boys have all fought in the ring.

'I didn't have a real boxing background as such. I knew about the old man and I knew about my uncle and the characters around at the time. My other uncle from south London was a good boxer too. I remember years ago when I was a kid he came in with a massive great pair of horse-hair boxing gloves and went, "Here you are, son, spar it up," so yeah, there were always those underlying tones, but the old man never fought pro or anything like that. He was game though. I can remember a time years ago at the fairground, one of the boys who worked at the fairground tried to throw me off a ride and the old man had a scrap with him. He's 76 now. Fit as a fiddle. He really can move.

'It rubs off too. I mean all my boys now – you see 'em in the gym; they don't train every day of the week but it's in the blood. It's even gone down through the generations to my other son; it's nothing to do with boxing with him – it's wrestling. He's 13 years old – he'll throw you up in the air; throw you over his shoulder. He's into the WWF.

'Unlicensed boxing is like an extended family, and it's good – we go in and we do our stuff and it's proper, you know?'

It was late and Jefferson's Bar and Grill was emptying. Alan left me the posters, the videotapes and his contact numbers. He said he would think about letting me film his next show. He had drawn me into his world and I wanted to see more. He still did not trust me fully and I still did not fully believe that his unlicensed boxing was completely safe. I wanted to see it for myself. I wanted to be let into his 'closed shop' of a world to see what it was like – and film it all, the good and the bad.

TWO

ALAN HAD INVITED ME TO HIS HOME TO VIEW SOME TAPES OF fighters. 'It's the house with "Jesus is Lord" over the door,' he had told me. When I arrived I noticed the sign painted on a semi-circular piece of glass that sat above the front door in red lettering with a black border. I wondered why the sign was there. Maybe Alan had bought the house with the sign already in place and he hadn't got round to taking it off. Maybe it was actually the name of a fighter he had once managed. I went through a number of weird thoughts about that sign. But all of them were wrong. Alan was a born-again Christian whose conversion was as abrupt as it was stunning.

The young, wild Alan drank and did drugs to excess. He would go on drinking binges that could last two or three days, on a regular basis. He wouldn't go home or contact his wife during this time. He would, by his own admission, have to go one better than his friends and this would drive him to do outrageous things. He had a particular party piece that summed up his attitude in those days.

Cattle prods are not the sort of thing you would normally take to a party. A bottle of wine; a case of beer, yes – but a cattle prod, no. Alan did. As the evening warmed up and the drink and drugs flowed he would gather people around him and put on his show. He would produce the cattle prod and say that he could take the charge, which was designed to stun a bull. There was always someone else in the group who thought that it was easy to take the charge on their chest – or perhaps they thought it had been modified or weakened in some way. But this was far from the truth.

Alan would let them mouth off. He would tell them about the dangers, the burns, the shock that could stop a half-ton cow and that it was seriously dangerous. The more he said they shouldn't do it the more they wanted to. Backwards and forwards the argument would go, them saying they could take it, Alan saying they couldn't, until it couldn't go any further and the talk stopped and the action had to start.

The cattle prod was charged up, its hum barely audible above the music. It was handed to the challenger and Alan told him what to do.

'Just touch your chest with it.'

There was a moment's hesitation. The challenger would be wondering how things had gone this far. But it had happened and there was no turning back.

Cattle prods are designed to give a shock to animals – normally cows or bulls – to make them go where you want them to. To half a ton of animal it was painful, but for a man it was almost unbearable. A weaker version of the cattle prod called the 'Tayzer' is sold in America as a self-defence weapon. It stuns an attacker, pushing him away and allowing the victim to escape. It's banned in this country. When the prod touches the skin it sends out a massive electrical charge that runs through the body. This is what Alan's challenger was about to unleash on himself.

It must have been a spectacular sight, seeing a fully-grown man thrown clean off his feet and flat onto his back, writhing in pain or literally knocked spark-out, his hair standing straight up.

Then it would be Alan's turn.

He would take a deep breath that filled his lungs and puff his chest out, brace himself and – *BAM*. Sparks would fly as the current shot through him. He took it and just stood there. This was an act that typified how the young Alan was back then.

Alan had a well-deserved reputation for violence that eventually earned him a prison sentence on the Isle of Wight. Prison, he said, was even worse than outside. They 'were serving each other up every day' (he makes a cutting gesture with his hand as if with a razor blade). A lasting painful memory of that time was when his wife had to bring their new-born baby to see him in prison. Laura had had to give birth without his support – he was not there to see his son born and the guilt of that absence stayed with him.

Exactly what Alan did to earn money at that time wasn't something that was part of our conversation but it was clear that he provided well for his wife Laura and his boys. His long periods of partying and his hopeless addiction to hard drugs and drink put an enormous strain on his marriage though. 'If I had kept going in the same way I would have ended up dead or serving a long prison sentence,' he says. It needed a miracle to change the situation. According to Alan, one came.

Laura was threatening to leave as she had had enough. Despite her desperate pleas for Alan to change he was too far gone to do it himself. In desperation she contacted an old friend, an ex-drug dealer who had changed his life by becoming a born-again Christian. He came to their home, and in the ensuing chaos and tears and laying-on of hands Laura herself was completely overwhelmed and passed out. She was peaceful, more so than she had been for many years and she found comfort in this instant conversion.

When it was Alan's turn he half wanted to believe the power of God could save his marriage. But too much of the old streetwise Alan remained. He did not believe. For him, saying that he did believe would only be a scam to keep his family, get rid of this unwanted guest and get on with his normal life. But that night Alan had a vision. He became a real born-again Christian. Literally overnight he stopped taking drugs and drinking alcohol. He has not done either since.

Now he tells his story to other people – villains, drug abusers, prostitutes, violent criminals and the abused. He tells them it was the power of Jesus that saved him. If someone wants him to pray with them he will do it, and if they want him to listen he does. I've seen him pray in gyms with boxers. He has prayed with people in cars, in other people's homes, in hospitals and in prisons. He's a born-again Christian but is not tied to any specific branch of Christianity. He and his friends take the bible literally and take its message out on the street to the so-called 'underclasses'. It's sometimes called 'street-religion'. Alan invited me to a prayer meeting. It was unlike any prayer meeting that I could imagine. It wasn't held in a church or scout hall, but in a field in Canning Town. Two vast white marquees had been put up in playing-fields not far from the A13. It was a hot, sunny day. Children were running about laughing, screaming and playing. Music thumped out from the marquees – not religious music, but house music. As I made my way towards it, the music stopped and was replaced with a familiar voice – Alan's.

He was telling the assembled crowd sitting there – people of all ages and colour – about his life – the violence, the drugs, the drink, his time in prison and finally how he had let Jesus into his life and had changed it all around. It was powerful stuff.

I stood at the back, enthralled, watching him talk. Some time later I realised I was standing next to a skyscraper of a black man who was also watching intently. He noticed me looking at him and I introduced myself. We shook hands, mine feeling like a child's in his. He introduced himself as Tom and he knew who I was. Alan, who was an old friend, had told him about me. We got talking and went outside where it was quiet. Tom then told me his life story which was as violent and as extreme as any I had heard. It is as chilling as it is simple and it still frightens me to this day.

'Ten years ago I wouldn't even be able to talk to you. I was too angry, too full of hate. I would have probably ended up hitting you – that's how wound up I was,' he told me. 'I was known for carrying a gun. There were no half measures with me – it was either fight or walk away – and I never walked away.'

But like Alan, Tom's life changed for the better suddenly and without warning. One night, Tom was in his usual spot in a kebab house in Ilford, his centre of operations. People would come in and order their large doner kebabs with chilli sauce and chips and Tom would take care of business. He was vague about the exact nature of this business, but he said it often meant he needed to carry a gun. On this particular evening he did not have it with him. A friend came into the kebab shop and started driving Tom mad, trying to get him to go to the Room at the Top, a nightclub above a department store in Ilford High Street. Tom had other things to do, however, and decided not to go. Disappointed, the friend and his girlfriend went without him.

Security at this club was strictly observed, with regular body searches. On this occasion, for some reason the men on the door picked out Tom's friend, who was an ordinary working man – not trained to fight and not looking for trouble. Tom thinks his friend was searched because they knew he knew Tom. There was tension between Tom and the firm of bouncers who ran the Room at the Top in those days. A bit of hassle between Tom's friend and the bouncers encouraged them to embarrass him in front of his girlfriend. The situation turned ugly, there was a scuffle and the girl got hit. The two were barred from the club. Angry and upset, the couple returned to the kebab shop to recover. Tom was still there. He was furious and decided that he would get an apology out of the doormen. He took the fire escape up to the back of the club.

Little did he know that as he ran up the stairs, his anger building, the bouncers had spotted him on the CCTV cameras and they recognised him immediately. They knew he was a handful so they were prepared for trouble. When he arrived at the top of the stairs a bouncer was waiting for him in front of the closed emergency-exit double doors. Tom wanted to get into the club and get an apology from the men involved but the bouncers wouldn't let him in. He was told to go back downstairs. But Tom stood his ground. He said he wasn't leaving until he got an apology. Suddenly the doors flew open and six or seven huge men armed with baseball bats burst through. They began smashing him to bits. His head and upper body took the full force of the blows. They battered him to the ground, but still they didn't stop, it seemed to go on forever – kicking Tom, punching him, again and again the baseball bats smacked into him. It must have been a terrifying thing to hear his own bones breaking inside his body. The bouncers carried on until they ran out of steam. Tom blacked out.

When the attack stopped Tom's head had been caved in, his skull was open, his eye was hanging by its optic nerve on his cheek, his face had been mashed to pulp and his jaw hung loose. Hardly any part of his body had escaped injury – his hands, legs, ribs, knees had been broken. But the internal damage was far more sinister. Scans showed an ominous dark stain on his brain. A life-threatening blood clot had formed. The surgeons could operate but they thought it was too dangerous and that Tom was too weak to survive it. They repaired what they could and left Tom to recover. When he left hospital his jaw was wired up and he was covered from head to foot in bandages. He ate through a straw and even when the wire frame was removed he could barely open his mouth.

There was no relief from the physical pain. No drug was powerful enough to remove it. Psychologically he was damaged too. Large chunks of his short-term memory disappeared fast. It fuelled his frustration and deepened his anger. 'All I was waiting for was to see them dead and then I would kill myself,' he said. Tom could think of nothing else but revenge. He ordered a contract killing, sat back and waited for the news that his enemies were dead and prepared to die himself. He could not live with the constant, unbearable pain. Tom's wife knew nothing of his plans. She knew he was in pain and felt frustrated and wanted to help him. At this point though, Tom was just marking time, waiting for things to end.

One day his wife organised an evening out with friends. Grudgingly and still in a daze, Tom went along. At the end of the evening he found himself at a prayer meeting hosted by an American evangelist. His wife had organised this in the hope that it would do him good. But it was the last place Tom wanted to be. He was not religious, did not believe in God and hated everyone.

'I didn't want to be there,' he said. 'All I wanted to do was get out. This was not for me. All I was worried about was hearing the contracted job had been done but all this guy was talking about was forgiveness.'

Tom was not even listening, or so he thought – but suddenly the preacher's words started to get through. 'It was like he was talking directly to me and no one else,' Tom explains. 'He said that there is a man in the audience who is in great pain, but that this would go if you just forgive your enemies.' This was the last thing Tom was thinking of doing – forgive nothing: they will be punished, he thought, and the sooner the better. But something extraordinary was happening to him.

'I was getting very hot, gasping for air, the pain was intense. I heard the preacher's voice and the next thing I knew I was on my feet. Everyone else was sitting down and I was standing but I couldn't stop myself.'

It was at that moment that he forgave the men that had beaten him up so savagely. It was no fake forgiveness either, he really meant it. Instantly the pain in his head began to ease, the temperature dropped and Tom was able to sit down again. He took out his mobile phone and cancelled the contract there and then. By the end of he evening the pain had almost completely gone. He was able to open his jaw much further than at any time since the beating and later even managed to eat an un-liquidised digestive biscuit. From then on, like Alan, whenever the time is right he tells people about his conversion to Christianity and how it saved him and prevented the death of others.

Tom is now 40 and owns a thriving business. He has a new baby girl and his life is better than it has ever been before. There are times when Tom is tempted to solve problems in the old way – when someone owes him money or offends him. On these occasions I imagine Tom bursting into a room with nothing on his mind but fighting to the death. He is capable of it, but the fact that he chooses not to do it is a testament to his strength and beliefs. The desire for revenge is taken away. (This story comes with a health warning for anyone who is thinking of taking advantage of Tom's turn-the-other-cheek policy, by the way. Beware – he has powerful, loyal friends who are not Christians – they will find you and will sort out the problem the old way!)

Walking back into the marquee with Tom I looked around and wondered how many others in the audience had had similar experiences. We watched as Alan finished his talk. Alan grabbed some sparring pads and asked if anyone wanted to come and punch them. Immediately kids of all ages rushed up and swung at Alan. But all the time he had his eye on something else.

Standing at the back were a group of tough-looking young men, aged between 16 and 19. They had an attitude about them and were laughing and joking, slightly disrespectful of what was going on. Alan approached one big kid standing in front of the others. They talked for some time and to my amazement Alan began to pray with the boy there and then in the marquee, two rows from the back, with children and adults milling around them. The others in the gang sneered and jeered at their friend and left. Undaunted, Alan kept praying. When they had finished the boy left, wiping the tears from his eyes.

'He's given himself to Jesus,' Alan said.

One thing is for certain: Alan and Tom's fearsome reputations as street fighters and hard men go before them. It is this that gains them access to some of the most deeply troubled people in their part of London. Alan's unlicensed boxing provides him with the opportunity of showing that you don't have to be weak to be Christian – you can be strong and fight in the right place at the right time, for the right reasons. You can be fit, streetwise, talk tough and still believe. Telling others of his street fighting and alcoholic past touches people in a way that no social worker, policeman or priest can.

For some of the people Alan meets on the fringes of society, life has taught them to be criminals; it has taught others to be victims. Alan and Tom's faith and boxing offers another way. Their particular swagger seems to provide another image, separate from those of gangsters and thugs that attract many people they want to help. They are not what might be considered typical Christians. They provide an image closer to home – they are Christians but in the past they used guns, razors, bottles, clubs and fists. They are tough, fearless Christians with tattoos and shaven heads. But don't let the 'Jesus is Lord' T-shirts fool you. They're hard. And their message is: if we were saved, you can be too.

There were many more things about Alan I was to find out – how he owned a club that was so much trouble that the police gave him a licence to run it just so that he could clean it up for them; how he constantly tries to improve himself and strives to do whatever he can for his family, and how he put on the biggest unlicensed boxing event in the East End for over 20 years.

I didn't realise what 'hard' really meant but I was about to find out. The Last Man Standing event had 14 of the toughest fighters to come out of London on the bill. It was three weeks away and it would be one to remember. I just had to be there to film it.

NATURAL BORN FIGHTERS

THREE

CHIGWELL IS ONE OF THE WEALTHIER PARTS OF ESSEX. ITS residents are made up of people whose parents or grandparents migrated from the East End to the countryside. Accountants, footballers, property developers and stockbrokers rub shoulders with shopkeepers, builders, car mechanics, second-hand car dealers double-glazing salesmen and a fair old smattering of villains. It is a quiet little picturesque town and it has its fair share of golf and health clubs. One of them is the Epping Forest Country Club. At various times it has been owned by such celebrities as Sean Connery and Bobby Moore, it's not the sort of place you would expect to find unlicensed boxing. But that's exactly where it goes on.

Driving through the huge gates and down the long tree-lined drive, there is a golf course on the left and a driving range and swimming pool on the right. The words 'up market' spring to mind. *The Sun* would describe it as a 'top-people's playground'. But the Atlantis bar, a nightclub owned by the club, and set in its grounds, has been plagued by bad publicity.

Fist-fights and stabbings have become increasingly common. The cause, it is rumoured, is drugs. Both Essex police and Waltham Forest borough council, who issue entertainment licences to the nightclub, have come under intense pressure to close it down. The club was fighting to keep the Atlantis bar open. Security has been stepped up but it seemed not to make any difference. Despite all of this the nightclub is still a popular place and most weekends it is packed out. An unlicensed boxing match with a crowd that could cause trouble and more bad publicity was the last thing the club, the police or the council needed. The Last Man Standing event looked as though it might be stopped. But at the last moment the council relented, and, with strict instructions not to allow more than 800 people through the door, and after assurances of tight security, the event was on.

Alan had eventually trusted me enough to recommend to the Epping Forest Country Club owners that I come and film the Last Man Standing event. So into this highly sensitive situation walked my film crew and I, preparing to make a documentary for Channel 5 about the underground world of unlicensed boxing.

Inside, the Atlantis bar smelled like any other nightclub the morning after the night before – it stank. Stale alcohol and urine made a heady cocktail. It was a big club with a sophisticated lighting rig, three bars and a large dance-floor. Alan's boxing ring had been set up in the centre of it. Around it, Alan's sons, Sean and Jamie, were busy arranging the chairs in order of ticket price: fifteen pounds for the back, twenty-five pounds for the middle and fifty pounds for the ringside. Trestle tables had been placed around the boxing ring for the judges, timekeepers and local celebrities. One was the infamous Roy Shaw, the man who started the whole unlicensed thing off.

Britain has always had a history of raw, uncontrolled, underground illegal fighting. Back in the '60s and '70s, it came from the fringes of society, what you might call the criminal element. Roy 'Pretty Boy' Shaw was born in east London in 1936. He was a notorious villain of the '60s, always using his fists. Roy has retired now but is still active in the boxing world. He's well respected by boxing promoters and fans and he is regularly invited to hand out trophies at events all over London at both unlicensed and licensed events. He, along with Lenny Mclean, are considered the godfathers of unlicensed boxing. Roy was there at the birth of big, openly advertised unlicensed boxing events in the UK. He learnt from an early age how to fight and just kept on doing it.

'I used to have the bullies after me,' Roy told me. 'And then after me dad died and they was still just jumping on me I just got fed up one day. I felt this adrenaline rush come right through me so I just started smashing away at 'em and they just kept falling over, so I knew I was blessed. It's a gift – a gift from God, you know, the power of a punch.'

That gift won Shaw many boxing honours but also got him into serious grief with the law. 'H' Stephens was the master of ceremonies and referee at a lot of Roy's fights. He says: 'Roy could hit. Oh, he could hit. Once he caught you – oh – *unbelievable* punches. He had about eight or nine professional fights, and he knocked every one out. Could have gone a long, long way, but unfortunately he got into trouble.' Roy got 18 years for armed robbery. Once inside, his reputation for violence earned him five years in Broadmoor. 'No one meant nothing to me,' Roy says. 'I've done two or three geezers at the same time 'cos of the adrenaline rush. I suppose it's a type of fear – it just comes up and I just ain't worried about nobody.'

In 1973 Roy came out of prison. He was known by the authorities as 'the most violent man in Britain'.

Roy says: 'I needed money bad and the only way I knew how to get money in them days was to go out on the blag or have a row. There was a fella who came over called Ronnie Smith, and he said, "Roy, come over to Barnet fair with me. Earn yourself a few quid." I asked him what he meant. He said, "Have it with the pikies over there."

'I had three bare-knuckle fights and got six grand. So that was the start of it. And then they mentioned Donny "The Bull" Adams, the "King of the Gypsies". They said "Would you fight him?" and I said yeah.'

Joey Pyle knew Roy from prison and recognised that he had a massive reputation among the criminal element. They would go anywhere to see the great man in action. In prison his fights were legendary. Outnumbered by prison guards, he would still take the fight to them. Joey could sell lots of tickets and make them both a lot of money.

Joey says: 'So he went to fight some gypsies. People told him, "There's only one for you and that's Donny Adams." I said, "Well let's do it properly, let's get some tickets printed up and make it a fight."'

Joey took the fight to another level with his marketing flair and sense of what the man in the street wanted. He created a huge carnival buzz around the fight and Roy could hardly believe it.

Roy says: 'Absolutely thousands of tickets were going 'cos we only had 'em at a fiver each. And I think every pikey and gypsy in the country must've bought one because we kept having to have more and more printed.' Amongst the travelling community the word was spreading and tickets were selling hand over fist. At fairs and in pubs the conversation would go: 'There'll be heaps of travellers going. Gang-loads. They'll come from the south, from the north, they'll even come from Scotland. Everyone's gonna be there to see this fight. And it's gonna be the best fight you ever did see, mush.'

It was turning into a huge event amongst the criminal fraternity too. To gangsters and wannabe gangsters it was the place to be. Dave Courtney, a young aspiring villain, remembers vividly what it was like: 'Yeah I was only young but I remember it. And so does everyone my age who lived in London at the time. Because it was as big a thing as the Kray twins going to prison, or the Great Train Robbery. It was something very, very exciting.' And one detail made it even more exciting. Joey and Roy had come up with a plan to make the fight an even bigger attraction for bloodthirsty fight fans.

'On the ticket we had "Fight to the death", which is illegal I suppose,' Joey says.

The police took both fighters to court. But the judge ruled that the match could go ahead, though the boxers had to wear gloves. There was to be no bare-knuckle contest between Shaw and Adams. But Joey Pyle had other ideas.

'The idea was to get all the fellas, after about the third round, to stand up around the front rows of the ring and join hands so the law wouldn't be able to get to the ring. Then Roy and Don would take the gloves off and start to tear into each other and the law wouldn't be able to get near.'

The fight was set for 1 December 1975 in the Big Top of Billy Smart's Circus in Windsor. By the time the night arrived excitement had reached fever-pitch. Roy was in the eye of the storm. 'There were thousands there, like 3,000,' Roy says. 'It was jam-packed – as many people as you can get in Billy Smart's Big Top.'

H. Stephens was there at the time and still remembers the intensity of the event. 'You had supporters of both camps getting into the mix trying to wind each other up. When Roy got into the ring he was in a very bad frame of mind. He'd been winding himself up. Never talk to Roy Shaw in the dressing-room. He was dangerous. Of course when the fight came to it and the bell went, it was like two tanks rushing at each other.'

Even today the fight is still talked about by those who were there, but Joey Pyle sums it up nicely. 'The bell went, Roy went across the ring . . . BANG! One right and it was all over.'

Roy recalls, 'Yeah, it was all over pretty quick. I was so fit and I had so much in me . . . I only hit him once and he went over. Then I was hitting him on the floor and kicking him, everything. I just had to get it out of me.'

A fellow unlicensed boxer, Steve Columbo, also there at the time, remembers: 'A few of his [Roy's] officials jumped into the ring and they stopped him because he went absolutely berserk. He jumped on Donny like an animal, punched him when he was on the floor and I think he was stamping on him as well. Everybody thought Donny was dead.' Adams survived, just, but something new had emerged from this event. The new 'unlicensed fighting' was born. Joey Pyle and Roy Shaw had unwittingly begun a trend.

Nosher Powell, ex-pro fighter and unlicensed boxing referee, sees them as the forefathers of this shadowy sport.

'The people that were behind Roy, realised there was big money to be made in this thing,' he says.

Local and national press had covered the fight. Donny Adams and Roy Shaw were interviewed on the radio and they even made it onto Eamonn Andrews' TV show.

'They made a big fuss out of things,' says Roy. 'People came round taking me photo and people were asking for me autograph . . . but then again at the end of the day I was just after money to build me house, so we had to get the next fight on and that's how it went.'

So that's how unlicensed boxing really came about, and its sons and heirs are alive and well today. In the next few hours we were about to see it in all its full-blooded glory at the Last Man Standing event.

Alan recognises the history of unlicensed boxing but has his sights firmly on the future: 'Well they were the guys that actually started it off. They were the glory days, the buzz days, but now it's a new millennium and *this* is what we're doing and it's exciting stuff.'

At the Epping Forest Country Club, Alan was inside the ring putting up the sponsors' ring-post advertisements. As he worked, his mobile phone rang constantly. Fighters wanted last-minute instructions about the time they needed to get to the club, others wanted free tickets, others wanted to buy tickets in advance and have them left at the door under their names. He barked out orders to his sons who immediately obeyed. A small army of maintenance men checked the lights, the sound system and the ring. Bar staff began to get ready for the evening, checking the beer barrels, making sandwiches and restocking the plastic glasses. The volume on the ear-splitting sound system was turned to the maximum, belting out gangster rap. Meanwhile the weigh-in area and doctor's examination room was being prepared.

Part and parcel of unlicensed boxing is an 'enthusiastic' and – shall we say – excitable crowd. And since half of the East End punters there had some connection to the fighters, keeping control looked as if it would prove tricky. But Alan had organised a top-flight security firm for the evening and they began to fit the two seven-foot-tall metal detectors behind the front doors of the club, where the crowd would come in. Other entrances and exits were locked, and checked by the growing number of black-bomber-jacketed trained and licensed security guards whose job it was to keep order in the club throughout the evening.

Geoff, a seasoned security guard, was on duty that night. At 6ft 6in tall (and about the same across), and with a handshake like a vice, Geoff was just the sort of man you needed at an event of this kind. 'Doing the door with the boxing is totally different from doing a nightclub,' he says. 'They get all worked up, they wanna see a row and see their man win. When he's losing the jeering starts, and if they're sort of firmed up – 15 to 20 of each fighter's mates – that's when you've got to play it very carefully. They're revved up and they're looking for blood basically.'

The Country Club was now filling up with fighters of all shapes, sizes, colours and creeds: vast heavyweights with pumped-up muscular bodies; thick-necked, short, squat fighters with arms as thick as your thighs. There were willowy young lightweights and thirtysomething middleweights with beer guts, and there were lean-looking men with sharp muscle definition mixing with hard, graceful athletes. They filed through the doors of the nightclub and made instinctively for the ring. They all carried large kit bags, some with the name of the gyms they trained at displayed across them – 'The Peacock'; 'The Averly'. Inside the bags was all the paraphernalia of battle: gumshields, boxing gloves, wraps, smelling salts, jockstraps, Vaseline, vests, shorts and boxing boots. Some fighters arrived with a group of people surrounding them: trainers, fathers, brothers and girlfriends. The guests headed for the bar and the fighters milled around the ring, shaking hands with old friends and old adversaries. But they carefully avoided eye contact with their opponents for the night. It was strange to watch; they knew exactly who they were going to fight and everything about them – weight and height; whether they were orthodox or southpaw; how many fights they had won and lost and who they'd been against. But they did not

NATURAL BORN FIGHTERS

acknowledge each other's existence. This was obviously part of the pre-fight ritual.

One fighter described the thoughts that went through his mind before a fight. 'Everyone wants to win and fighters always think that they are going to win – if they don't they've lost before they get into the ring. If it's not to be, if they don't win, they pray they won't look like a mug, or look too stupid in front of their equals, their family and friends. To lose face is painful, more painful than getting a broken nose. At least a broken nose will heal. Losing face lasts a lifetime. If they lose they want to lose well, to a good fighter; a hard fighter with a good reputation. If they get knocked out it has to be with the hardest punch anyone has ever seen. It sounds mad but that's what its like for most of these people.'

These things are in the mind of every fighter before he climbs the steps, slips between the ropes and gets into the ring. It's part of what he feels before the bell goes and all hell is let loose. Doubts and fears pop into the mind – it's natural, they get the adrenaline pumping and their bladders filling – all unspoken fears. It's the mind telling the body *not* to put itself in danger, it's 'flight or fight'. Every fighter standing there in the Epping Forest Country Club talking, laughing and whispering was having these thoughts but they would never admit it.

One fighter who was on the bill that night was Tiger, from Edmonton in London. Tiger told me: 'I'm 28 and light middleweight at 11st. I think I've had about twenty fights and lost two. My opponent has had a good few fights – he's no fool apparently. I'm just looking forward to getting this on. Obviously I've heard all the talk, how he's gonna come and knock me out, but it's all talk, the usual talk before a fight. I ain't getting togged up with that. Action speaks louder than words. Tonight we'll see what's what. It will be a fight, I can tell you. I don't fall down for no one.'

Tiger had once trained in America with professional boxers and so what, I asked him, is the difference between unlicensed and licensed boxing?

'People wanna come and see blood spilt . . . There's that bit more blood and guts to this [unlicensed boxing] I think. The referee will let you get away with a little bit more too. There's a lot more of an aura around this as well. That way you'll sell a few more tickets, if people see a good show they're happy. If they go to a show and it's just a bit of tit for tat they don't want to know. They like to see a war.'

Tiger got into boxing when he was very young – eight or nine years old. His father took him to fights and boxing practice. He then did his real fighting in America for seven years. That's where he learnt the game; the tricks and skills and the science of boxing. He was training with professionals. He had no fights, just training. It took him all around America. Tonight, Tiger was fighting Paul Kavanagh.

He says: 'I heard what he was talking about in the gym on the "gym-to-gym telegraph". Stories travel. Whatever he's got in his bucket, he's got. I have my own plan. We'll see. There's no gym rivalry really, it's all between him and me in the ring. We'll see who's got what it takes. I want to win and I've got every bit of bad intention for him for the fight. After that, let's have a drink.

'I'm ready for it. For this fight or for any fight I train twice a day but normally I keep to once a day. I couldn't do every day, twice a day, I'd kill myself! In general I train every day, five days a week to tick over. I need to train or else I'd go mental.

'Unlicensed fighting is not like your "on the cobbles" fighting. I think they're trying to make unlicensed boxing as professional as they can now, to be honest with you. I love my boxing and I can't box professional so this way I can do what I love when I want – that's it. But to me boxing is my game and in many ways it's similar if you get into a boxing ring with a licensed fighter as it is with an unlicensed fighter – same tactics, same stamina, same techniques and tricks, the same game of chess. There's a lot more to it than just getting out there and having a fight.

'There is no difference with mental attitude or the way you feel when you get in the ring at this event or a pro event – it's the same. You've got to have your head right. You can't go in there just feeling fit. You've got to be strong and be able to think strong. You've got to have a good boxing brain too. So it's not my idea to get in there and just have a tear-up because you're not going to last long like that. You have got to know your game. Okay, in unlicensed the referee will let you get away with a little bit more. But it's not like bare knuckle, which is a hard, hard fight. Every bare-knuckle fight you are going to be cut up and there's going to be a gruelling fight no matter what. You are going to break your hands and get cut to pieces, and if that happens it normally doesn't last too long.

'When I found out about these shows I wanted to be involved. I thought – yeah, this'll get me back into the ring. I went to one, then I find out about the next one. Once you are in the game you throw links out to everybody and soon you find out when the next one is, and how they work. Its all done by word of mouth. When you're at the fight, pride and ego take over, you want to get in there and win. You want to be that macho guy.

'I'm giving everything to this fight. I'm not working because of it. I'm doing nothing right now except training. I cut out everything else. Afterwards, I'll go back to working the door. To win in the ring gives you that little bit more confidence [as a bouncer] on the door, that little bit more. While that other guy is thinking about having a go, it's already over. That's how I like to do it. While the thought's in their brain – it's already end of story, you know? Through training and sparring you are that little bit more awake. On the door you are getting a lot of drunk people trying to have a go. But when you are a very fit man you're wide awake. It's not really a fair fight, being up against a man who knows what he is doing.

'That's the other thing about the unlicensed game – you get work from it. Someone sees you and asks if you can look after his pub or if you can come and sort out trouble. Through my boxing, through that reputation you get from fighting, I have been given jobs on the door and debt collecting too. And that's what it really boils down to – reputation.'

Tiger continues: 'My old man loves it. They are always worried about me, as any family would be. But they all look forward to it. I think they've got enough belief and confidence in me to know I'll be all right. I'm pretty sure they know I ain't got no worries and anyone around me ain't too worried about me either. They'll be here today shouting for me. I've sold a few hundred tickets. People want to come and see blood spilt and with this fighting you are going to see just that. So that's what it's all about, really. People want to see you get knocked out and people want to see a bit of blood and guts at the end of the day.'

One of the whips makes an announcement.

'Can all the fighters come over to get a medical please?'

Tiger walked over to the doctor. He took his T-shirt off and the doctor asked him if he felt well. We all laughed. Here was a man who looked like he had been sculpted out of marble. He did not have one ounce of fat on him. Plates of hardened muscle covered his whole body. He had been training every day for the past two months and running five miles every other day. The question seemed stupid but it had to be asked. After listening to his heart and taking his blood pressure, the doctor passed him as fit. Next was the weigh-in. He was on and off the scales in seconds and his weight was perfect. In unlicensed boxing the opponent is asked at this point if he still wants to go on with the fight, the reason being that it may not be an even match with the heavier fighter having the advantage.

Tiger grabbed his bag and made his way to the changing-rooms upstairs, which were being shared by everyone who would fight in the red corner. With him came Darren his trainer, and his friend Wayne. As we moved towards the changing-rooms more and more people were coming through the doors of the club. The music was now on constantly and the atmosphere was becoming increasingly tense.

In the changing-room a continuous stream of people came through the door to greet Tiger and wish him luck. Every time it opened the booming music invaded the room. Soon the Tiger supporters left and the small changing-room quickly filled up with fighters, bags and trainers. There was then another change of mood. It got a little more serious and suddenly there was less joking. The fighters were beginning to change. There was no time to talk to camera crews now – it was time to get ready to fight.

Floyd De Front, a small, solid, dark-haired fighter was already changed and warming up, throwing punches out at an imaginary opponent, his trainer encouraging him, urging him on. 'That's it – *good* – keep it short and sharp. Relax. Keep your hands up, keep moving. Don't give him an easy target to hit.'

Someone came into the room and as the doors opened, the noise from the nightclub downstairs was a shock; only half an hour before the place had been empty. Downstairs the people were finding their seats, ordering drinks, shouting to friends across the room, laughing and joking.

Watching the dressing of a fighter is like watching a knight having his armour put on. He stands in silence while others prepare him for battle. He puts on his own jockstrap and shorts, and the calf-length 24-hole boxing boots. I stood watching Tiger having his long hair braided into a ponytail and watching his corner-man Darren smear the Vaseline over Tiger's eyebrows, cheeks and chest. It was a well-rehearsed ceremony. They wanted everything to be right for him. Fighters have minimum protection but what they do have has to be comfortable. The binding of the hands, the Vaseline, the lacing of the boots. To me it seemed more like an ancient religious ritual that had been practised for hundreds of years than preparation for a sporting event.

Wayne, a giant of a man, well over six feet tall with bulging biceps, was binding Tiger's hands with red wraps. There's an art to wrapping a fighter's hands to give them maximum protection without cutting off the circulation. Even though they are protected by thick, padded boxing gloves during the fight, hand bones break. While Wayne wrapped, Tiger gave him instructions to loosen this bit, tighten that bit, put more round the thumb. When the wrapping was finished Wayne used masking tape across the knuckles and between the fingers, making a tight package of Tiger's hands.

When the preparation was complete Tiger stood there – black hair; long, black shorts; laced-up red boots; red, bandaged hands and his body as tight as only someone's who has been doing serious long-term workouts can be. He then began the next phase, the warm-up.

He literally shook off all the stiffness from his joints. He stretched his neck muscles, swinging his head from side to side. He flicked his feet out, loosening his leg muscles. Then he raised his arms and began shadow boxing, slowly at first – short, stabbing uppercuts to the left and right. Gradually he built up the speed, his fists always returning to barely two inches from his nose. Soon Tiger's shoulders began to work more freely, the tension from his neck released with every volley of punches into the air. Wayne helped him put on the bag gloves (padded gloves used specifically for pad and bag work).

Darren slipped his pads on and Tiger focussed in on them. Darren held his hands up and barked orders at Tiger.

'Left jab.' One instantly shot out and smacked into the pad. 'Right jab.' The right shot out from the shoulder and hit the target with a thud. One–two. Tiger let fly with a relaxed right and left jab then an uppercut. Knees bent slightly, he dipped his body and brought up the right fist, elbow bent. Again the pad thudded with the blow. The momentum built up: one, two, three, four jabs. A right hook, a left hook, an uppercut. Blood was now rushing to the parts of Tiger's body that needed it most. Every time he hit he deliberately grunted and this forced the air out of his body. All boxers and martial artists do this. It's part of the preparation for being hit. Blow the air out of your body and the muscles stiffen. If you're hit your body is hardened for the blow. Tiger was building up a rhythm now, and with the rhythm came power. The punches were getting harder and faster, but they were also still loose and relaxed. When his hand shot out it was almost like he was catching a fly. Hand open until the last moment when he made a fist on impact. His momentum built, Darren's orders got faster and Tiger instantly responded. Left, right, left, uppercut, uppercut, right hook, left hook, a double. Then it stopped. Tiger sucked in air, shook his arms and paced around the room.

There is nothing like the smell of the changing-room just before a fight: the mixture of BO, menthol smelling salts and sweat-stained leather. All the fighters along with the camera crew that day generated a lot of heat as well – it was stifling in there. After a while, though, you get used it. Suddenly one of the whips burst into the changing-room.

'Floyd, you're up next son, get ready.' Immediately the fighters gathered around Floyd, touching gloves and giving words of encouragement. Floyd's trainer led the way out of the changing-room, his corner-man behind them. The door opened and they were gone.

Four fighters were left crammed into the small changing-room now – all at different stages of the pre-fight preparation. Trainers spoke to fighters in whispers, quietly going about their business. From downstairs came the music, and the crowd chanting a fighter's name that we could not hear. There were shouts of encouragement – ''it 'im you wanker!' – mingled with whistles and boos. The entertainment was underway. Floyd was in the ring and he was fighting, but in the changing-room a humble hush had descended.

We stayed with Tiger as Wayne helped him pull on his boxing gloves. He washed his gumshield in water and popped it into Tiger's mouth. He then slipped a white poncho over Tiger's head and the warrior was complete. The whip came in and called him down.

'Tiger – you're up next!'

Wayne lead the way out of the changing-room and immediately as the door was opened the volume of the music hit us like a smack in the face. Its bass thumped through us. The noise of the crowd was stunning.

Wayne, Tiger and Darren filed down the narrow staircase and waited in the corridor by the toilets. The smell of stale piss stung our nostrils and made us want to heave. But Tiger paced up and down the corridor taking deep gulps of the foul air. We could see the crowd but they could not see us. As Floyd came back in, sweating and with a red blood blister closing his left eye, we heard the announcement from Steve Holdsworth, the Master of Ceremonies, standing in the ring. He called Paul Kavanagh, Tiger's opponent, to the ring. Paul's music started booming out fast and hard and through the open double doors guarded by two security men at the other side of the club 60 metres away, we could see Paul's head bobbing up and down. Leading him out of the far holding area reserved for blue-corner fighters was Alan Mortlock, his trainer and coach. His corner-man was backing him up.

I didn't know Tiger or the man he was fighting, but I still felt nervous and secretly wanted Tiger to win. It seemed like an hour before Steve Holdsworth called Tiger to the ring. His music kicked in: 'Eye of the Tiger' belted out, and the crowd began to chant his name. T–I–G–E–R, T–I–G–E–R, T–I–G–E–R and as they chanted they stomped on the ground. Tiger didn't move. He remained focused and still he waited. The chanting continued, the song was in full flight and still Tiger held his ground.

I wondered if Tiger had had second thoughts, perhaps he couldn't move from the spot and didn't want to fight, or perhaps he'd forgotten how to walk. But this was not the case. It was part of the mind game fighters play. Keep the other guy waiting, let him worry about what you are doing, dictate the pace of the fight even before it starts. Well that's the theory anyway.

Finally Tiger nodded to Darren and Wayne and they all began to move towards the double doors. The security guards talked into their walkie-talkies and moved into the crowd to make a path for the fighter. The crowd nearest the doors were on their feet. They saw Tiger and they all screamed his name. The stomping and the chanting got louder as more people caught sight of him. Kavanagh's supporters started their own chant; the clash of both sets of supporters in such a small place created a tidal wave of noise. Everyone was on their feet. The blood and guts that they wanted to see was not far away and nor was the man Tiger was fighting. Paul Kavanagh, the 'White Destroyer', was waiting in the ring with Alan whispering encouragement to his boy.

Paul is slightly shorter than Tiger and he's lean and compact. He also worked on the doors of clubs and pubs. He wore Union Jack shorts and, like Tiger, he was going to fight bare-chested. They were perfectly matched and yet completely different. Tiger's long, dark, braided hair contrasted with Paul's short, cropped blond hair. Almost every muscle of Tiger's was visible; Paul's body was smooth, his definition not so pronounced. Tiger smouldered with aggression and pent-up anger; Paul was calm, focused and determined. Suddenly Tiger looked smaller, more vulnerable than I had first thought.

Steve Holdsworth left the ring and Gary Bedford, the referee, was now in charge. He called the fighters to the centre and they stood six inches apart, staring each other out, neither one wanting to back down or look away. Darren stood behind Tiger, Alan behind Paul. When the referee had finished his talk to the fighters they touched gloves and returned to their corners to wait for the bell. Neither of them sat down. The timekeeper ordered the seconds out and sounded the bell.

Tiger came flying out of his corner and for the first 30 seconds just kept throwing punches at Paul, keeping him on the defensive. Tiger slammed a low, hooking right hand into Paul's ribs, who tucked his elbows in and covered up, preventing the blow from hitting its target. But before Paul could throw a counter-punch, Tiger followed up with a left hook to the other side of his body. Again Paul covered up and protected his body. Tiger smashed a right-left combination to the head but Paul's defence was sound. Nothing got through, but he was shocked. Tiger kept coming, throwing punches to the body and then switching to the head. Paul had to cover up and defend, he couldn't fire off his own shots, but he refused to go backwards, he commanded the centre of the ring. Tiger was the more aggressive fighter but Paul had not been hurt and Tiger was expending valuable energy. Still he poured in every sort of punch – uppercuts, hooks, jabs, body punches, head punches. Paul soaked up big bombs of punches, he covered up and pushed forward, trying to close Tiger down. Tiger backed off giving himself room to swing more punches into Paul's body. Paul was battered and hadn't even thrown a punch, and looked confused.

The crowd screamed for their fighters. Tiger's people urged him to finish Paul off. Paul was looking worried, wanting to strike back and make it through the first round. Then for a split second there was a pause in the barrage. Then Tiger came in again, swinging a wide arching right hook. Paul had seen it though, and for the first time he backed off to give himself some room. He stuck out a straight right jab into Tiger's face and followed up with a thunderous left hook to Tiger's jaw. Tiger fell backwards into a corner and as he pushed himself off the ropes he sprang back right into the path of an incoming right hook. Somehow Tiger saw it coming though and ducked under it, moving in close. Paul countered that by covering up and pushing Tiger away. Tiger stumbled back and Paul pressed on, launching two massive left and right punches that landed on Tiger's jaw. Tiger was still standing but stunned and Paul kept coming – a left and a right, another left and a right – all of them hit home but somehow Tiger kept standing. His mouth was open and he took yet more punches to the head but still he didn't go down. From somewhere he dragged up the strength to hit back. Two strong hooks shook Paul's head and he came back with two of his own, his mouth open too. Technique had gone out of the window – this was nothing like chess! Both Paul and Tiger soaked up each other's punches and gave their own back. They were hitting each other simultaneously – as Tiger's left landed on Paul's chin, Paul's right landed on Tiger's chin. It went on for punch after punch – there was no defence from either of them, just attack.

The crowd were on their feet, pushing forward towards the ring, willing their men on. 'Kill 'im!' a woman behind me shouted – who she meant I didn't know. Darren pounded the canvas with his flat palm, trying to get Tiger to cover up and defend. In the other corner Alan screamed at Paul to keep the pressure on.

The two fighters pounded each other but Tiger was on the back foot. He sensed (more than he saw) that he was being backed up into the corner and with a magic piece of footwork he turned a massive right cross from Paul into a miss. Paul almost flew through the ropes

NATURAL BORN FIGHTERS

43

and out the ring and Tiger saw his opportunity. He slammed right into Paul's ribs. Paul winced but came straight back up and jabbed his way out of trouble. The pace slowed but the punches kept coming – big punches with power and each fighter slipped them, moved, and set himself up for his own shot. Not one punch was weak or wasted. Both men had taken some hard hits and survived them, they were still thinking, counter-attacking and trying to make every punch count right up to the bell at the end of round one.

Everyone took a deep breath. The tension and excitement carried into the short break, people hurried to go to the toilet, rushed to get drinks, not wanting to miss the next round. All around the crowd relived the most dramatic parts of the fight so far. Tiger's girlfriend cuddled her friend, the excitement too much for her.

In the corners Darren and Alan worked hard on their men, giving them drinking water, replacing Vaseline on swelling eyes and cheeks, massaging tired muscles and giving last-minute instructions. Tiger took big gulps of air, Paul took big gulps of water and they stood up waiting for round two to begin.

Time was called again: 'Seconds out, round two.'

It started as the first round finished, with both fighters hammering into each other blow for blow. Tiger let fly with a ramrod straight jab and followed up with a ripping uppercut. Paul took the jab full on the nose. It jerked him back, but he stubbornly held his ground. The uppercut was blocked but blood spurted out of Paul's nose, hitting Tiger in the eye and mouth. Tiger blinked, and it gave Paul the split second to regroup and crash in a right hook. This time blood poured from Tiger's nose. They clinched and Paul worked inside Tiger's guard, thudding short, sharp uppercuts into Tiger's ribcage. They hurt. And then the course of the fight changed. Tiger saw red. He held onto Paul, turning into his body. He tilted his head back and BAM, he head-butted Paul. I saw it, the referee saw it and the crowd all sides of the ring saw it. Paul pulled away and the referee stepped in, holding Tiger in a neutral corner. Tiger wanted to apologise, instantly regretting what he had done but it was too late. Blood gushed from a gaping cut above Paul's right eye. All hell broke loose. The crowd screamed abuse and booed and whistled. Alan pressed a white towel on the cut to stop the blood and to allow the referee to look at it. It was the pivotal moment in the fight.

The referee stopped the contest and briefly looked at the cut. He asked Paul if he wanted to continue and Paul said 'Yeah!' This was what Alan meant when he said that they went a little bit further.

The fight was back on and now Paul was angry. He wanted revenge and in the ring that can be fatal. They touched gloves and instantly Paul went to work. It was payback time. Tiger stood toe-to-toe with Paul trading punches but he realised that he was coming off worst. He back-peddled and Paul went after him. Tiger was up on his toes, moving about, making Paul miss. He sidestepped an over-extended Kavanagh cross which left Paul's side exposed. Tiger hammered into him with a combination of two short, stinging shots to the ribs. These hurt Paul – and it showed. Tiger had found his second wind. He was moving around Paul, picking him off with strong, solid punches to the body. Paul looked flat-footed and now Tiger was almost smiling.

Paul sensed he was losing ground. He dug deep and caught Tiger with a flurry of punches. Suddenly it was Tiger who was overwhelmed with this onslaught that Paul was mounting. He seemed to be running out of steam when seconds before he was on top. Paul was chasing him all around the ring now. Tiger was fighting back but was on the retreat and Paul seemed to be drawing strength from Tiger's weakness. Again and again Paul attacked. Style had gone out of the window now, he was gambling on one last-ditch volley of punches to finish Tiger off. This was all heart now – Tiger was still standing; Paul was using his last reserves of energy, sensing that Tiger was going to go down any second. But still Tiger kept standing.

The crowd were on their feet again, pressing forward towards the ring. Darren and Wayne were up on the apron of the ring, hanging over the top rope. Alan was also there, urging Paul to finish the job and all their fists were pumping the air. Tiger's mouth was open, gulping. His hands were down, but still he threw punches, although

NATURAL BORN FIGHTERS

they had no power. Paul's face was contorted with pain. His lungs burnt but still he kept piling the rights and lefts into Tiger. He was in control, sensing that if could just keep going Tiger would fold.

When the end came it was not a killer blow that finished him. The referee judged that Tiger was out on his feet, unable to defend himself. Tiger didn't know if it was the end of the round, the end of the fight or the end of the world. Suddenly he was surrounded by people. Wayne and Darren jumped into the ring, annoyed that it had been stopped. Alan was already in there protecting Paul. Both sets of supporters were shouting and climbing on the apron of the ring – one group celebrating, the other complaining that it was unfair. It looked like there was going to be another fight in the ring between the supporters of both camps. Then Tiger broke away from Wayne's massive arms and made for Paul. He hugged him and held his hand up in a gesture of respect and honour. This action broke the ice, and the seconds, and the trainers left the ring. The crowd settled back and the announcement was made: Paul was the winner in the third round. Alan was jubilant. His fighter had shown courage and strength and both fighters had produced a classic battle, raw and bloody – just what the crowd loved.

Back upstairs, in Paul's changing-room, Alan was patching up his man. He told me: 'I would say that that fight was as good as any professional fight, but in the second round Tiger "nutted". He put the head in and cut Paul. The referee stopped the contest briefly to look at the cut and asked if Paul wanted to carry on and go for it, and Paul said "Yeah!". Possibly in a professional show they may have stopped the fight. So if you like, yes, we go a little bit further, but obviously there was no kicking, punching or anything happening on the floor. They was boxing.'

Paul was over the moon. 'I knew I was gonna win, I *knew* I was. That's why I said to the ref. "Don't disqualify him, I'll fight." Did you see the reaction of the crowd? Did you see how they was all off their seats? They loved it. You don't get that much at a pro fight. They're buzzed. I got no grudges, do you know what I mean? If it happens, it happens.'

As for Tiger – well, he was disappointed but happy. 'I can't complain. I should have boxed and used my head. I didn't. I listened to my heart instead of my head.'

So the crowd got their war, Paul Kavanagh fought on to victory, and the White Destroyer tamed the Tiger. But upstairs in the gym two more fighters were warming up – Manny 'The Maniac' and 'Gypsy Boy' Defries had their own war planned and it wouldn't be long before hostilities started all over again.

FOUR

MANNY CLARKE IS WHAT YOU MIGHT CALL AN UNLICENSED fighter from the traditional school. He is also a doorman with a reputation and a heart as big as a bear's. The thing about reputations is that you have to earn them. At some point you will be challenged and when you are challenged, how you react and act in the face of danger determines how you will be viewed and known for the rest of your life. If you back off and run away you will be known as a coward; if you stand and fight but lose against overpowering odds they will say that you are as 'game as a bagel'. If you drop to your knees and beg for forgiveness you will be forever known as a mug, someone who can't stand up for himself – not the sort of thing you want said of you if you make your living by fighting.

Manny's moment of truth came out of the blue on an apparently regular night on the door.

He says: 'I myself haven't fought for eight or nine years. The last time I boxed, I boxed amateur. I've always stayed around the gym, done a bit of training here and there and I'm known to the boxing game. I heard a friend of mine, Hughie Robinson, was doing unlicensed boxing and he was doing pretty well, so I phoned him up and said: "I fancy a go."

'I don't know much about the guy I'm fighting. All I know is they call him Darren "Gypsy Boy" Defries. He's had a few unlicensed fights. I don't know if he's had much of an amateur career or anything like that. But I've seen a few of his fights before and basically I think I'll beat him.

'I've got a lot of people coming down to see me but I wouldn't class it as a really big fight. But it's going to be a good fight. Apparently Defries is a tear-up merchant and loves to come charging out for a row. He likes a big fight, which suits me. I prefer them to come tearing at me because I'll be able to box round him and beat him. I think I'll be able to stop him.

'I box heavyweight but I'm only 5ft 10in. Usually most of my opponents are taller than me so what I'll basically do is I'll dominate the centre of the ring and I won't go back and I'll do most of the work. I've got a very big left jab, an excellent left hook and a heavy punch with both fists. I can knock people out with either hand.

'I've got loads of family. I've got five kids and three of them are coming tonight. I've got four brothers coming too – my dad, my mother, everyone, you know? They all like it. Most of my family have boxed. My dad did. He had a very good amateur career. My Uncle Freddie boxed professionally, he had about 150 pro fights in the 1940s. He boxed Bruce Woodcock, Freddie Mills and people like that. So we're used to it in our family.

'A lot of boxers pace around and start shadow boxing and all that. But you'll probably see me lying on the floor until it comes to my fight, then I'll come walking out and I'll warm up when I get into the ring. I can't be bothered with all that standing in front of a mirror and shadow boxing. Of course, every fight you have, it doesn't matter if it's your first fight, last fight or whatever – you're still going to feel a little bit nervous. Nerves get you through the fight, though. They make you a bit more wild when you get in there.

'When I come from the dressing-room to that ring what I'll try to do from that moment on is blank my mind out and think of nothing. I'll try to ignore the crowd, who are going to be going absolutely crackers 'cos I've got about four or five hundred people there who have come to see me fight. And they'll be screaming and going berserk. What I've got to do is ignore that and just completely blank my mind. I'll go up those steps and focus me mind on me opponent. If I come out there shaking people's hands and all that, I'll probably step into the ring and get knocked spark-out. That's what usually happens if you don't focus yourself.

'Basically I find that boxing actually gives you a lot more confidence, and keeps you a much calmer, more placid person. I run a security firm and we supply bouncers and I work on the doors right across London and the home counties. It's good for you, it keeps you fit, makes sure you keep your wits about you. It keeps you on your toes. You're used to having things chucked at you, and you know how to move out the way!

'You've got to expect trouble in any crowd you're working in; you can't underestimate any of them. If people play up, you drag them out the door. You speak to them nicely and you do your best to be very polite and diplomatic and if they're not fucking polite and diplomatic back, you just drag them out the door. But being polite and nice to people usually works.

'During the build-up to the fight, people are at their peak of fitness. Some of us here have actually got quite bad tempers – not me, but some boxers do have bad tempers and they do fly off the handle a little bit. It's nothing personal – and we're all good friends really.

'Basically I don't do too much before a fight; I relax. I stay in, have early nights, go to bed about nine, ten o'clock and just sit indoors. I take no chances that I might go out and have a drink, have an accident, break my hand or anything. I just do nothing and just relax 'cos all our training's done by this time and any more training that you do will only slow you down and leave muscles tense or unrelaxed for when you get out in the fight. Basically you need to be as relaxed as possible when you get out there and step up into that ring.

'You can feel the fitness and the strength oozing from you. Alan makes sure of that. He handles things very well. He's good to us lot, you know, he's always there for us a million per cent in training. If you're fighting for him and you want to train at any time or whatever, he goes out of his way for you and really looks after you. He's a nice fellow.

'It takes a lot for any man to actually get up into that boxing ring whether he's amateur, professional or unlicensed. You get a lot of people who sit there in the crowd shouting "Yeah, knock him out, punch his head in!" But they couldn't stand in that fucking ring on their own, you know? They're all right sitting there with all their mates behind them but it takes a very serious, determined sort of man to get up and do something like this.

'My mum will be going absolutely hysterical, she always does that. You'll probably hear her, she'll be the noisiest person there. She'll be sitting on Mortlock's table and she'll be screaming like mad. She does martial arts, my mum. She just goes mad whenever she sees any of us fighting in the ring. But she's seen me in worse situations – much worse, this is nothing.

'I got stabbed four times in a club in Essex. I was working as a bouncer there. I got stabbed four times in a punch-up – and I got 18 months in prison for it. They nicked me for violent disorder because I knocked out most of the cunts who did it. I got stabbed in the back and twice in the side. At the hospital they had to cut me open from my chest to below my belly-button and they had to take my spleen out. I was stabbed in the face too – in the cheek, just on my jaw-line. When I woke up in hospital I was handcuffed to the bed with the police round me and *then* they nicked me!'

Manny stood in front of the camera posing in his Thames Bookmakers-sponsored T-shirt, stared straight into the lens and said: 'Yeah, that's right – it's Manny Clarke, I'm *Manny Clarke.*'

Alan called Manny a warrior for the new millennium. He says: 'Manny's gonna be the total fighter. He's fighting for the All-London heavyweight title in September. He's got such a huge following – it's unbelievable, they're coming from all over the place, it's very exciting.

'I met Manny through a mutual friend. He gave me a bell and we

PRIORITY ORDER FORM

☐ Please start/renew my subscription to *Classic & Sports Car* and send me my free mini maglite

YOUR DETAILS (BLOCK CAPITALS PLEASE)

Mr/Mrs/Ms _____ Name _____ Surname _____

Address _____

_____

_____ Postcode _____

Telephone _____

email _____

I wish to receive offers via sms and email ☐

DIRECT DEBIT DETAILS

Instructions to your Bank or Building Society to pay by Direct Debit

To The Manager: Bank/Building Society _____

Address _____

_____

Postcode _____

Name(s) of Account Holder(s) _____

Branch Sort Code ☐☐ ☐☐ ☐☐

Originators ID No. 850699

Bank/Building Society account number

☐☐☐☐☐☐☐☐

Reference Number (for office use only)

Instruction to your Bank or Building Society

Please pay **Haymarket Publishing Services Ltd** Direct Debits from the account detailed in this instruction subject to the safeguards assured by the Direct Debit Guarantee. I understand that this instruction may stay with Haymarket Publishing Services Ltd and, if so, details will be passed electronically to my Bank/Building Society.

Signature(s) _____

Date _____

Please return this form to the address on the right.

Terms & Conditions: Offer open to UK subscribers only. All applications must be received by 31st May 2004. Responsibility cannot be accepted for applications lost, delayed or damaged in transit. Please allow 6 weeks for receipt of your first issue. Offer is subject to availability. If stock runs out you will automatically be given 3 free issues and then charged at the advertised rate. A copy of the Direct Debit Guarantee will be sent upon request.

Overseas rates available on +44 8456 777 821

054DI

We may use your contact details to inform you about other offers and reputable companies, whose products and services may be of interest to you. Please tick this box if you do not wish to receive such offers ☐

NO STAMP REQUIRED (UK ONLY)

CLASSIC & SPORTS CAR

FREEPOST
SEA14710
Haywards Heath
RH16 3BR

(This address can be used on an envelope)

started from there. We did some work together, hit it off and never looked back. Manny is the main man in the heavyweight division.'

Alan bandaged Manny's hands and put extra bandaging on the left one. He then got him moving around, shadow boxing, shouting instructions: 'Nice and relaxed . . . move about. Nice and loose, move yer head! Nice breathing – deep breaths. Jab. *Jab*! One – two – three . . . left hook! Over the top! Double-jab, right hand over the top . . . move that head. Under, over, under, three punches. *Good*. Weave under my hand and *hit*. I want three jabs now . . . one, two, three – knock 'im out! TIME! Okay. Sweet.'

Someone walking through the door of the gym caught Alan's eye and he immediately introduced him to Manny. 'Manny, this is Steve Columbo, old-time unlicensed boxer.'

Steve Columbo's real name is Steve Richards. He speaks with a thick mid-European accent. Despite living in London for over 45 years, it's stayed with him.

Manny worked around the small, matted area of the gym, moving slowly and keeping his muscles loose. Steve talked to him and Manny seemed to relax, his mind off the fight for a few minutes.

'I came here after the Hungarian Revolution. I escaped in 1956 after the uprising. I came here from Austria. We were in a refugee camp for two months. Then I made the decision that we should come to England. My earliest memory of boxing was from Hungary in 1944 or '45 with my uncle who was in the Hungarian Championships. I was 14 and I walked in and put my right hand up as defence and my opposition left himself open so I knocked him out with a left hook in the Amateur Championships. Soon afterwards people kept calling me Columbo but I didn't know why. I think it was my general look.

'There was a plumber working at the British Council and he asked me to come and do some training in London and that's how I started as an amateur. In 1960 I visited the Battersea Amateur Boxing Club. After I joined I won the South East Division Welterweight title and soon after I turned professional. I had my first fight here in 1960. But professional boxing, in my opinion, is fixed. I was a pro on and off eight years, so I know. When you go out there to fight, you think of nothing else but beating your opponent.'

And with that Steve Columbo turned and left. A slightly confused and distracted Manny resumed his warm-up. Columbo slowly hobbled out of the gym and took his VIP ringside seat next to Roy Shaw. Quiet music drifted up from downstairs and spread a serene atmosphere over the gym and the fighters. Fighters stretched and breathed deeply, the wraps were put on them and they were massaged.

Manny was moving about now and beginning to sweat. He took off his Lonsdale sweatshirt and jogging bottoms, revealing a pair of shimmering gold lamé boxing shorts, complete with tassels. Alan had also changed his clothes. A black martial-arts top now covered his black T-shirt, a Christian fish emblem on the back. Manny put on a towelling robe, while his old sparring partner Tommy March spread Vaseline over his body. Soon his yellow 'Title' gloves were on and he was skipping from one foot to the other, throwing out loose punches.

Alan asked him if he felt good.

'Yeah, I'm ready to fucking rumble,' Manny replied. He took deep breaths and Alan called him over. It was time for the serious stuff – praying.

Alan placed one hand on the back of Manny's head and one hand on his shoulder. He pulled Manny's head forward over his left shoulder. Around them fighters stopped and bowed their heads out of respect. Alan, with his eyes closed, began to talk.

'Power him, strengthen him, Lord, give him power in three rounds. In Jesus' name, touch him, power him, let him be the victor, Lord, I don't want no man hurt, I want this man to *win*, in Jesus' name. Amen.'

Manny thanked him and said 'Amen'. Then his face changed and he gritted his teeth – no smiles, no jokes. This was serious. Manny was ready to go.

Darren Defries, 'Gypsy Boy', was also ready to go. He was not as smartly attired as Manny, and was wearing a white Marks and

Spencer's vest, black boxing shorts and high, working-man's boots.

As the whip called Manny to move downstairs they heard Gypsy Boy Defries being called into the ring. Manny's people moved en masse out of the changing-room, Alan leading the way.

There was the announcement – 'In the blue corner, from Malden in Essex . . . Darren Defries!' A monstrous beat crashed out.

Alan drowned it by shouting encouragement at Manny. 'See that jab of yours – working like a steam hammer, *bang, boom*.'

Then Manny was called.

'Representing Mortlock's Gym . . . Manny the Maniac!' His music boomed out. Alan waited until the music built up to a crescendo. Then he moved Manny to the doors and held him there. Manny's 400 supporters screamed his name. Still Alan held him in the same position.

'Wait there!' he said above the noise. 'You gonna do the job?' he shouted at Manny.

'Yeah – I'm gonna do the fucking job!' Manny shouted back.

'You ready?'

'Yeah I'm fucking ready!'

'You want this, don't ya?'

'Yeah I fucking want this!'

Then Alan led him out. The crowd went mad. They were on their feet, clapping and cheering as soon as they saw him. Manny held his concentration – there was no waving to the crowd or his family. He got into the ring, took off his robe and Alan slipped in his gumshield. He focused on his opponent and no one else.

Gary Bedford, the referee, called them together. He said he wanted a good, clean fight and wished them both luck. If Manny heard him he did not show it. He stood there as stiff as a board, his eyes boring holes into his opponent's head. Gary sent them back to their corners and they stood there, waiting for the bell.

The bell went and Manny crashed in with body shots. Darren was crouching, covering himself up though, so Manny was not getting through. His shots were hitting Darren's arms and elbows. Then Darren straightened and stuck out a right jab straight into Manny's nose. Blood spat out but still Manny kept coming forward. Then, again, Darren dipped low covering up and Manny slammed into his arms doing no damage. Suddenly Darren lifted his head and began to swing wildly at Manny. But Manny took the shots and kept driving forward, trying to hit back but missing. This initial flurry had tired both men. They circled each other taking in huge gulps of air and not throwing punches. The bell sounded for the end of round one.

Into the ring stepped the ring girl – petite and pretty in a bikini top, tight hotpants and thigh-length leather boots. She smiled and walked round the ring to jeers and whistles. Both fighters were taking instructions in their corners. Their people worked hard, giving them water, applying fresh Vaseline and rubbing arms and legs.

The bell went for round two and the noise from the crowd lifted again. Manny raised his hands and stuck out a slow left jab. It glanced off Darren's head and Darren grabbed it. Manny couldn't move and he was now facing Darren's back. He could only do one thing from here. He pounded the back of Darren's head with his right hand – but still Darren wouldn't let go until the referee split them up.

Darren began to dance around the ring but Manny cornered him and let go a massive right hook. After it connected, Darren bent so low that he almost kissed Manny's knees. Manny backed off to give himself room and got caught by a wild right hook that he didn't see coming – but this didn't move him. He led with his left and again Darren grabbed it, pulling Manny off balance. Manny's cheek crashed into Darren's head as he went down.

So the rhythm of the fight was established. Manny kept pushing forward, pushing out jabs and Darren kept covering up, bending very low and occasionally peeking out to launch a wild attack on Manny. But he just would not go backwards. He stood there like a rock, they were toe-to-toe with each other. Manny would swing a left and right at Darren who would immediately cover or grab Manny's arm.

The bell sounded for the end of round two and wolf whistles rang out again for the ring girl. Manny's corner worked to take down the swelling on their man's right cheek which was ballooning fast. In the other corner Darren's team were telling him the score was one all. There was one two-minute round left to go.

The ring girl, tottering on her high-heeled boots, climbed shakily out of the ring and the bell sounded for the last round. Manny stood up quickly. Darren waited. Both men looked exhausted. Their hands down, they danced around each other, both launching attacks at long range at the same time. Manny kept sticking out jabs, Darren would stumble backwards into the ropes but he couldn't seem to follow up with his right hand, then further jabs. Darren backed into the corner. The crowd were on their feet sensing that if Manny could just use that big right hand of his he could stop Darren in the last round. But he just couldn't. Darren slipped out of the corner and back into the centre of the ring. Manny was drained of energy now, his arms dropped completely. Luckily Darren felt the same. He had no desire to come back in for more.

But eventually Manny pushed forward, as he had done earlier in the fight, for one more attack. He hit home with that left jab and Darren stumbled backwards. This time there was no rope to help him. Still, somehow he managed to stay on his feet. But Manny could not follow up. He braced himself to carry on. Suddenly the bell sounded and Manny cuddled Darren in a victory embrace. He knew he had won.

The referee and the judges confirmed it. Nothing less than a win for Manny would have been any good and he'd got it. He stood in the centre of the ring, his hand held high by Gary Bedford the referee, the swelling on his cheek almost closing his right eye. Along with the twisted grin it made him look a bit like Popeye. But it had been a good night's work and he was delighted with the result.

FIVE

ROY SHAW HAD BEEN CLEARLY ENJOYING THE EVENING FROM his ringside VIP seat and after he had given out the belts I was introduced to him by a mutual friend. Being one of the most famous 'natural born fighters', I asked if he'd mind if I interviewed him – my programme wouldn't have been complete without Roy. He said he'd be happy to be involved and invited me and the crew to his home in Essex, not far from the country club.

Later that week we arrived at his house – a beautiful bungalow surrounded by fields and forest. Roy made us feel very welcome and was more than happy to talk. When Roy Shaw speaks, everybody pays attention. He started by recounting his days in the unlicensed boxing ring and told us how he came to be such a big name in the game.

'I had a professional licence under the name Roy West and I was fighting for Mickey Duff then. But I got that while I was on the run from borstal. When I got home I got nicked and they gave me three years. So when I came out, I was still only young. I tried to get me licence back and they wouldn't give it to me, which was a downer because Mickey Duff said I was one of his best prospects around at that time. But they knocked me back so I went on to robbing banks. I could have made me name as a professional fighter, though.

'After I got out, one time I fought Ron Stander who'd come over here from America. They're top heavyweights over there, they don't play around with them. They're a different level to us – bigger, more hungry. Anyway, Ron was always out with Terry Downes getting drunk every night and clubbing it. He wasn't training properly. He was kicking the bag and jumping around. One time he slipped and hit his ribs on one of the rings that holds the ring post and hurt his ribs. I didn't know this beforehand, but he still turned up for the fight with me.

'So I was getting in some lovely, lovely punches, you know? Really banging on, and he was saying, "That's it boy, keep going, keep it going." I couldn't believe it. It wasn't as if I had to run after him to do it, he was a big lump and he was just standing there. He wasn't tall like Lenny McLean. So I was crashing him full on. I've never known anybody stand up to it like that. I just had to keep banging away. And all he kept saying was, "That's it boy, keep it up, keep it up." When I went back to me corner, I says, "He's taking the piss" – you know, I couldn't hurt him. But they kept telling me, "Keep going, keep going."

'And so I went out again, and I slung a right hook, right up into his belly and he went "*Umphh* . . ." And I thought, oh – that's the first sign – and so I just keep smashing away under his left rib and he fell through the ropes. But he got back up in time so we were straight at it again and I kept hitting him up into the ribs. Eventually he fell out the ropes again but this time he didn't get back in time so they counted him out. But if it hadn't have been for that bad rib of his, he'd have really hit me. He never really hit me with a good shot because I was tucking up and keeping it soft. For the first time ever I boxed a bit sensibly. Ron Stander fought for the world title so you can't just go in and bang away as though he was nothing. I was picking me punches. But if he'd have hit me I would have just gone. He was in a class way above me.

'We was all in the papers and on the news and that. I was a bit of a celebrity, really. People walked in and they went "That's that Roy

Shaw, that's Roy Shaw!" They were all from street level, you know, people from my own background. I might walk into a place full of stars or something and they wouldn't know who I was. But at street level, people knew who I was. I had a lot of respect that way. Everybody treated me well. I'd go to any of the big clubs where most people on the street couldn't get in. So it was nice like that.

'It was a shock really, because before this, when I was lying in my prison cell for years, I'd never have thought that I would be in the position I am now. I've got me money now and as I got older I used my head with property. Suddenly it all fell into place. I had a lot of luck. You need luck in business or property. I'm on me feet now. I'm as happy as anyone can be.

'My biography *Pretty Boy*, written by Katie Kray, was a number-one bestseller. You can't get better than that. And now they're talking about making a film of it so that'll mean more publicity and small-time stardom.

'I've been to a few unlicensed events recently. But they haven't really got anyone special. See, when we were doing it, they had me as the main event and then you had challengers who wanted to knock me off me stool. We had loads of other good fighters on our bill too, and that made up a good bill and the atmosphere was absolutely electrifying. It was like a reunion as well 'cos I had a reputation in prison from doing a few screws and I was always in loads of trouble in there. So everyone who knew me from prison who'd got out was coming. They would come up to me and then they'd go, "Hello, remember me from 1943?" You were meeting people all over again.

'So it was all them people that packed my fights out at first. Then word of mouth just went round, we'd get more packed and more packed. The geezer who ran 'Sinatras' [where the fights were held] was saying "No more! If the fire people come I've had it. No more, tell 'em no more!" But as soon as he'd gone, we let 'em in. I mean everybody you let in was charged fifteen pounds a head and in them days that was quite a nice bit of money. So we just packed 'em in.

'We had some good fighters with us – there was Patsy Gutteridge,

Columbo, Joe Lazarus, Mickey May, they were the main men who were on our bill nearly all the time – blinding fighters. And whoever challenged them knew that they had a war on their hands, you know? They wouldn't go down without having a good fight.

'There was one time, though, we got a call from Ireland, from people who wanted to put up twenty grand. They said there was this fella who was knocking everybody out over there. They said he was vicious. We had a meeting with him in a pub over at Notting Hill Gate. I was there, and was getting a bit worked up and excited. All of a sudden, they come in. They walk through the door and this little Irish kid was at the front.

'I said "Where is he then?"

'He said "I'm here." *This* was "Mad Dog Muligan". I told them, right, the fight was on – only 'cos they was putting up the money.

'So at the fight we saw him warming up. He was skipping, the sweat was streaming off him. He was knackered before we got in the ring. I'd never seen anything like it. He really wasn't what he was supposed to have been. But you know, the money was there – that was what it was all about. He was a nice fella. Afterwards he said, "Jesus Christ, sir, you can punch!" But he was very jovial and that.

'In our day anything went. But in licensed boxing both then and now you can't hit 'below the boot laces'. With our fights there wasn't a lot of real harm, there was a bit of nutting, a bit of low punching, but there was never really anything severe. I suppose it made it exciting if anything went on like that. But you know, people more or less stuck to the rules because they were all ex-boxers, you know? If you're a dirty street fighter, though, you'll go straight in with your head.

'We had people like Ronnie Redrupp and Cliff Fields. They were two of the top fighters. I wouldn't fight Cliff Fields. He was a big, powerful heavyweight. When he was fighting as a pro he was knocking everybody over. The only thing was that he used to get cut a lot. So he pulled out of the professional ranks and came into unlicensed fighting. But no one could live with him.

'I'm only really a middleweight, you know, blown up from bits of training and that in the nick. So I wouldn't even chance myself against him. I think he would have beaten me.'

Roy has his own views on unlicensed fighting today. He says: 'Now they've all got their own personalities. They've got charisma and flamboyance. Alan [Mortlock] has the music for one thing. And he introduced the girls into the ring for another. He's hot with all the young men and their wives. And it's a night out for them. It's a meeting place as well as an event. But they do really need someone who's a bit special – then they could have him topping the bill all the time. People would go especially to see him, then it might work better. I've been a couple of times and they've been good fights, though. They're packed out too. Their ticket prices are a lot lower than ours were and it's more glamorous. But to me it ain't got the same power as when we were doing it. I mean we even had the Boxing Board of Control scared, so that's how popular we was. I don't think they like me very much – well, I don't like them a lot either.'

Times have changed as far as Roy's concerned. Even the villains have changed, according to him.

'I think it's worse nowadays. There's more rascals about now . . . not rascals, mugs. There's so many mugs around now on cocaine and the gear and they're taking liberties. They're going out in gangs and beating people up for more money for dope. There was none of that in my day. I mean we went out and done blags but – well – they're covered by insurance, aren't they? We never hurt nobody really, honestly. But nowadays it makes you sick – you read in the papers that they're beating up and raping old women. It's because they're out of their box on the gear. Well, it ain't my scene and I think it's just going to get worse. We're about ten years behind America – perhaps five – and they've got loads of drug and race trouble over there. I think it is something that's going to happen over here.'

Roy's seen the effect of the changing times up close and first hand. He tells me: 'Me own grandson's in prison now. Four or five of them were out of their boxes and mugged a man. What's the matter with them? That's not right. He was just a straight man, minding his own business, going along the road, doing nothing and they jumped on him. You learn respect and that makes you a better person. If they had respect they wouldn't be taking people on. They wouldn't be abusing girls or whacking kids or people who had nothing to do with you. I would say the best thing you could do is to have respect for people and get it back from them and it'll make you a better person. But you have to earn it.'

In many circles Roy has now earned that respect. With his bestselling biography and also exhibitions and television programmes featuring him, he now has his own fan base. He remains very humble, however, and can't believe the attention he receives. He's even become a sort of agony uncle for some people.

'I find it very surprising that people write to me,' he says, 'why would they write to *me*? You get frightened people. I've had so many people write in to me saying, "I wish I was like you. I wish I could have done what you did because I've been bullied in the past." And, you know, how do you tell 'em? They're asking me what to do. What can I say? I can't advise them. I don't know how to answer them properly. I haven't got any extra knowledge, I only know what was right for me at that time, you know? I'd love to help 'em though. Maybe all I'd be doing is increasing their problems. They might end up getting done themselves. I mean I *was* aggressive. They'd come at me and I just used to flare up and bang 'em. But I paid for it. I lost all me remission in the prisons because the screws used to say something to me and I used to go "bang". I'd lose my temper completely. So if I told people to do that, to go and do the same thing, they're going to end up getting into trouble. So I can't really give 'em that advice, can I?'

I was grateful that Roy wasn't giving out that sort of advice and I moved swiftly on to talk about something else Roy does know about, and happily offers advice on – training.

He says, 'I still train four days a week. I go running in the forest every morning with me dogs, so I am fit. I'm training all the time. I like being fit and if I had to have a row in the ring tomorrow, I would be ready for it. The training gets harder as you get older but I'm still doing it.

'When I was living in Dagenham, I used to run round the parks, on the roads and then up to the gym. I was up there nearly all the time. Then I started going to one in East Ham. We'd all spar with each other there. When you go in to spar, you ain't in there smashing each other to pieces; you're learning about timing and distance and all that. There was no individual trainer for us unlicensed people. We just used to mix in and spar with anybody. If the pros wanted someone to spar with, we'd do it. And that is the main ingredient of a fighter's training. The more sparring you can get in – the more road work – the better. That's all you need, really.'

Realising time is moving on and that I might be outstaying my welcome I put a final question to Roy – how does he feel about his life now?

He tells me that he feels 18 years old. 'They say when you go into prison your brain stops and when you come out, it starts again. So you find that a lot of people who've done a lot of bird are very immature, you know? Well, I'm only about 18 with all the bird I've done. I mean, look at Frankie Fraser. He must be 75 or 76, something like that. But when you talk to him he jokes about like a youngster.

'I still go out with the old school, I can lay back, talk and have a good night and everything's all right and stable. If I have a good night, I have a good drink and don't worry about anything. That's the difference between then and now.

'I'm pleased with what I've done. I'm quite happy as I am and things will just go on that way. I've earned me money and everything else and it's down to the fighting. So even if the Board of Control never did give me back my licence – I got all this from fighting. I'm one up on them.'

What a perfect way to end an interview. Grateful for some wonderful insights into the mind of one of the most famous unlicensed fighters, I made my exit and wound my way back through the Epping Forest. Our next location that day was Chelsea Harbour.

SIX

TRAVELLING AT SPEED THROUGH THE COUNTRY LANES TOWARDS the M11 southbound, we were up against the clock. We had to get to the other side of London in 40 minutes – not an easy task. And in this game you can't be late. It's not respectful. And if you don't show respect you don't stand a chance with these guys.

We were on our way to the offices of Joey Pyle. Joe is another fighter who has earned respect. He was Roy Shaw's promoter in the glory days of unlicensed boxing – a man to be reckoned with. Driving into the beautiful riverside development beside the Thames it was clear that this man was a success.

Joey started boxing at about ten years old. He went professional, had a few professional fights, a couple of which he lost, but the rest he won. But he also fought in booths in fairgrounds all around the country. A smartly dressed, eloquent man, he told me about his boxing days as we sat out on his balcony overlooking the Thames.

'It was a good life, a fit life. A lot of it was "get-ups", they were "fixed". This was when you would take it easy when you were boxing, like in the booths in the fairground. "Straights" came in now and again and that was when you weren't taking it easy with the other fellow and he wasn't going easy with you and there was no acting. But when you're starting at 11 a.m. and finishing at 11 p.m. and you might have, say, four fights in that time, you couldn't have four *straight* fights a day, could you? Not six days a week.' He laughs.

So how did Joey move from fairgrounds to Chelsea Harbour?

He says: 'I started getting into promotion when the Board wouldn't give me a licence, back then I was promoting a fellow called Arthur Brookes, as a professional. But the Board got hold of him and said: "Look, you'd better get out of it, we don't want you involved with Joey Pyle," and so that was that. Then Roy came out of prison. Roy Shaw and I were really outside of boxing back then. I was just going round the gyms and doing a bit of training and keeping in touch with fighters and all my pals in the fight circiut. Then one day Roy said to me, "All I know how to do, Joe, is fight. I ain't got a lot of money," and next thing I know, he wants me to get him a fight.

'We ran "unaffiliated" shows. They've always said that when you do something unlicensed it's like it's illegal but on the other hand you never hear of an "unlicensed" football match, do you? Or an "unlicensed" cricket match. So why should you have an unlicensed boxing match? I was unaffiliated to the Boxing Board of Control – which was just a cheeky title they gave themselves. The British Boxing Board of Control – they're just nothing, really. They're just a body that controls the boxing, but they're not appointed or recognised by a court of law. They're self-appointed, self-elected. Anyway, they said I was unlicensed. But if what we was doing was unlicensed, then the law would've stopped us. That's how I look at it. But we were allowed to go ahead as long as we put a referee in the ring, as long as we had gloves on and we named the number of rounds that we was gonna fight. Things were run just as well as they were anywhere else, but the Boxing Board gave us this "unlicensed" bit.

'If you're doing anything they call unlicensed, what do you assume? It wasn't illegal at all. Anyway, I was only interested in it when Roy Shaw was boxing. I wasn't interested in bringing back fighters that were finished. The crowd wanted to see Roy Shaw because he was a guy that was a game fella from the nick. He had a lot of respect from the chaps, so that's what they wanted to see and they paid to see him. They knew that when they saw him, they'd be getting value for money. That's why they went to see him.

'Roy sure could draw in the crowds. We would pack out Alexander Palace with 2–3,000 people every time he fought. You couldn't fit anyone else in the place. It was just a thing we did together. He was the fighter; I was the promoter. We started off the so-called unlicensed boxing!

'Roy and I go back 30 years now. But we didn't intend to go that far. I just wanted to promote Roy and make some money for the both of us and for charity, which we did. For instance, two kids needed money to have their eyesight restored. We decided to put on a show to raise it for them. They got the money and went to Russia for an operation.

'Some of the rules we fought by were our own rules. It was rougher. That was the difference between the professional boxing shows and the shows they went to see at our place. They didn't wanna see two fairies in the ring. People go to fights 'cos they wanna see fights. If they see a good show, whether it be under Boxing Board of Control rules or not, they're happy. They like to see a war and that's what Roy Shaw gave 'em. He gave 'em a war. He was value for money and everybody liked it. Everybody went to see him. There were a lot of film stars, celebrities and musicians there. It's the same as going to see boxing at Wembley. Why should it surprise me more to see them all in there at my show with Roy Shaw rather than going to Wembley to see Henry Cooper, then? It's still boxing.

'Don't forget, these men had a reputation. If they didn't you wouldn't have been able to pack the place out. When Roy was fighting Donny Adams, who was the first one, a hell of a lot of people there thought Donny Adams would win. Then he fought the Irishman, Paddy Mullens, and the place was full of Irishmen. And then there was another guy who was going to fight with Roy called "Psycho Dave". Yeah, he was well known in the West End as a doorman, a hard man. But he pulled out of the fight but the tickets still sold because Roy was gonna be there. There was a huge following.

'Nowadays I like it, I think it's great. It's well controlled, it's well run. Any boxing's good though. Roy goes to all the shows. He wouldn't just go because the show's unaffiliated. He'd go because he just likes the boxing.

'Unaffiliated boxing has still got a place. I don't go to see it so much anymore but we just love fighting. I mean, that's in the man, isn't it? Why? It's something inside you, isn't it? I think there's something else there too. We don't look at boxing and just see two guys in the ring slugging it out. We see the training what goes into it, the dedication, the denial. To be any good in that ring, you've gotta deny yourself. It's discipline, that's what you see when you go to a show and you see two fighters. You see the fitness and everything else that's gone into it, you know what I mean? It's all put into that one night.

'It's not like bare-knuckle fighting. To me, I've got no time for that at all, because it's boring to watch. People think it must be good but let me tell you something – if you're fighting another fellow and it's bare knuckle, you've gotta hit him and then pull your head back. You can't walk in with a left hand and come under to bob and weave like you would if you had gloves on. You've gotta hit the guy and step back, because if he hits you, counter-punches you, he'll rip your eye open. So all the time you're going in and jumping back again. It's either a case of steaming in right away, in which case it's over in seconds, or it's tit for tat, jab and move back. So what do you want to see that for? If you're fighting that way, your knuckles would go, your hands would break.

'People love violence. Look at movies. People are still going, and the more violent the film, the bigger the audience. They're moving more towards violence than in the older days and there's more violent films out now than then. There'll always be boxing. They'll never stamp it out. And if they did stamp it out legally, then it'd become unlicensed and would go underground but you'd still get it. There's always gonna be that competition between men. And it's far better to put it in the ring, than out in the park, say, where innocent people can get involved. If it's in the ring with gloves on, they're not hurting anybody else except themselves.'

Joey gave us a look which said 'OK, filming's over' and as he did so he told us: 'I just love boxing, always have.'

SEVEN

BACK AT THE EPPING FOREST COUNTRY CLUB THERE WERE THREE
more fights to come. One of them was Roy Shaw's own son, Gary,
who was up against Chrissy Morris, who was the darling of the
crowd. It was going to be a grudge match just like the good old days.

Chrissy Morris, 26, is one of the renegade fighters on Alan's bill
and he had done his homework on Gary. He said, 'He's a very strong,
"walk-forward" type of fighter like myself, a good brawler and a
strong man. He's got a good chin. He's a nice little package of a fighter.
He'll definitely have a go – we'll stay in together all day and knock
lumps off each other. The crowd will love it and hopefully I'll walk
away the winner.

'His last fight got called off a little bit early 'cos he got cut. It's a bad
way to win a fight, no one wants to win a fight on cuts.

'If a fighter's family's got a bit of history it makes you think that
there's a good bloodline of fighting there. You know without a
shadow of a doubt that Roy Shaw was The Man in his day and Gary's
a good fighter as well. To be honest with you though, when the bell
goes and you're in the squared circle it's just you, him and the referee.
So reputation doesn't really come into it.

'Yeah, at the end of the day it's a family honour thing – you don't
want to let them down. You might be a good fighter, but your dad was

a good fighter, and his father before him was too. That's what you worry about. To be honest with you though, boxing's an upfront game. A lot of people would be intimidated knowing that his dad was a good guy and that obviously makes him a good guy but that's no reason to hold back. You go into a fight to win. When you get into the ring you've got to do your best. You know, it's just one of them things. You gotta deal with it. If you can't you shouldn't be in the ring.'

Chrissy had his thoughts on the others in the game. He says: 'Basically most of the people you meet in the unlicensed fighting game would probably fit in quite well to a Guy Ritchie film – like *Lock, Stock and Two Smoking Barrels*, *Snatch* and things like that. At the end of the day most of the fighters know each other, we're all mates really. But having said that, you get the grudge fights as well. When you go to a show you probably know most of the people that are watching. It's all nice and friendly. But there's still an edge there, you know? Basically most of the people around the unlicensed boxing scene here will be cockney wide boys, but they're rough diamonds really.

'I try and be nice to everyone and I don't rate myself. Most fighters that can fight don't need to prove it. They don't have to walk around throwing their weight around or anything like that. That's for people who are a bit unsure of themselves. They have to show the world that they can actually have a fight. It's just bravado. Whether I'm on the cobbles, in the ring or whatever else, I don't actually have to prove it. I'm a great believer in the idea that you should treat people the way that you want to be treated yourself.'

So what does Chrissy think makes a fighter?

He tells me: 'If you've got fighting in your blood you can't be a fighter one minute and something else the next. You have it running through your veins, from birth to death. If you're a fighter you'll stay a fighter. All the different types of fighting – whether it be boxing or some martial art – anything like that, if you've got it in your blood then basically you'll be a fighter for the rest of your life. Most of the fighters will perhaps have a criminal conviction for a little fight they've had when they were young or whatever. Often when you're younger, you don't know how to control yourself properly. As you get older you calm yourself down and you can learn to deal with your vicious streak a little bit better.

'Most of the guys will have tough jobs – doormen, something like that; some sort of security work. What you'll find is that most of the guys are sort of throwbacks to distant times, you know? Most unlicensed fighters should have been gunslingers in the Wild West, or gladiators in Rome, something like that. What I think is that as society gets more technical and there are more computers in the world, it pushes the fighters out. You no longer need to live and die with your sword, as you used to have to in the old times. Basically, fighters today are in the wrong century. We should be part of centuries past, along with medieval knights in shining armour, that sort of stuff – hacking people to bits and whatever else. Everybody needs some sort of release at the end of the day. If you're a fighter and it's in your blood, you got to have a way of getting that out. Obviously, no one wants to walk round bashing people for no good reason, but after mutual agreement, it's fine to get into a ring with another fella and have it out with him.'

So if these fighters fight because they *need* to fight why not go down the amateur route? Chrissy says it's not for him and that unlicensed beats amateur boxing hands down. He says: 'In amateur boxing you slog your heart out. They don't appreciate you, your punching power, or anything like that. You can have one fella running around the ring and someone else chasing him like he's a thief for three rounds and the second guy still loses. Even though that's the guy who's gunning for it the whole fight – just 'cos the other guy's ruffled his hair up a little bit, a few more times, the decision goes his way. Amateur boxing don't suit me at all. All you get at the end of an amateur boxing fight is people turning their noses up at you and some leftover food that some of the crowd don't want. It's just too political. I'd rather go to an unlicensed show, have a laugh with me mates, get in there, have a bloody good scrap and as you're coming out the ring, get a few pats on the back and "Well done son." Win, lose or draw, you know the crowd loves you. It's a good atmosphere, a good place to be, you know you're appreciated for who you are. At all the amateur shows that I ever went to, if you weren't part of the club that was managing the show it wasn't a nice atmosphere. They'd look down their noses at you. I'd stop a boy on an amateur show, knock him out, and for the rest of the show rather than saying, "Well done, that was a good knockout," they'd turn round to me, look at me like I just walked in with a bit of shit on my face or something. That's why I ain't a fan of amateur boxing at all.

'I did have a short-lived amateur boxing career, but I don't like the way amateur boxing is set up. I want to go to a fight, have my fight, have a laugh and be congratulated. I've been to amateur boxing fights before where I've stopped the guy I'm fighting – against the odds 'cos I've come out of nowhere and they've thought, "Oh, he's a new boy, we'll put him in," and they've expected me to get stopped. When I've won, rather than say, "Well done, you fought well," everyone just turns their noses up at you and treats you like a leper. That's not what fighting's about, you know? There's gotta be some respect.'

Unlicensed boxing gives Chrissy what he wants from a fight. 'I'm a boxer solely out of choice. I don't do it for any other reason than the fact that I love like the fight game. I've fought under different promoters in all sorts of different fights and different sorts of disciplines. But basically unlicensed fighting is the most upfront fighting you'll get. There's no politics in it, no frills. Most of the time in unlicensed boxing you're not having to chase the other fellow round the ring looking to land a punch. Most of the time you'll be in a slightly smaller ring, so it makes like a better fight. You gotta fight people and you can't run away from them. The crowd all like that a lot more. The rounds are usually a little bit shorter too. And less rounds means you got to put a lot more into that space of time. If you fight six rounds you'll spread yourself out over those six whereas if you have four or three you got to put double the action into half the time. And usually that's what the crowd see, and what they enjoy.

'I've been through amateur boxing, professional boxing, unlicensed boxing, kick boxing – you name it – and I do think the best atmosphere is at the unlicensed boxing fights, 'cos basically all the seats are sold to people who've got a *real* interest in the fight. Basically pretty much anyone that goes to an unlicensed boxing show has been before and knows what they're getting. The venue's got a lot to do with it too – if you get a nice venue you'll get a nice atmosphere. But an unlicensed boxing show is the best value around. You're getting two stand-up fighters, with no dilly-dallying, no frills, no silly stoppages or anything like that. Basically that's what the people want.'

One of the main differences between licensed and unlicensed fights is the attitude to weights. In unlicensed fights, if your opponent's weight is too much over yours, you'll be given the option to fight or not to fight on the night. But weight differences don't seem to bother Chrissy.

'I weighed in on my last fight at just under 11½st. I'm not sure what Gary weighed in at but he was heavier. If I know the fighter and I'm confident that I can beat him, the weight's immaterial. If Gary walks in at 14st that won't be a problem for me because I'm fighting him as a person. He won't be good at 14st anyway. Gary's best fighting weight is around the 12st mark. My best is around 11¾. If he has a little bit on me, it's not a problem. If it was the other way round, I'm sure he'd be all right with it too. There are some fighters, though, who won't give away any weight at all, some fighters who'll argue about a kilo here or a kilo there. On some other unlicensed shows, some shows where Alan's not been involved, I've given away what other people say is a ridiculous amount. But the way I see it is that, with both professionals and amateurs, if they've got to make strict weight limits they often dehydrate, and that's where you get medical problems happening – through dehydration. I'll walk in the ring, happy as Larry, with a little bit of food in me belly. I ain't bothered if I've got to drink a bit of water before I get on the scales – what I weigh is what I weigh, as long as I'm happy at my weight, basically, that's what matters. If you're happy with your weight and you've not drained your body too much you could fight all day pretty much. It's only when you dehydrate and lose too much weight that you start having troubles.

'If Gary weighs a little bit more than me, it's not a problem. He might come in 12½ maybe. I'll probably be just under the 12¼st, but that's not a huge amount of weight to give away. But hopefully I'll walk out there and have a win and then no one can say that the weight was a factor!'

Chrissy is confident and charismatic and Alan likes a fighter like him on his bill. But it goes both ways: fighters like Chrissy like to fight on Alan's bill too.

'Alan is a top geezer, a lovely bloke. He's an East End wide boy and I've known him for years. He always looks after the people who look after him. He don't stop for the shows you know? I'll phone him up a couple of days beforehand and I'll say, "Are you all right, mate?" and he'll go, "Chrissy, a hundred mile an hour, son," and I'll say, "If you need any help, I'm only a phone call away." He'll go: "Much appreciated, son." He's got his heart in the right place and he's definitely got the best intentions. Basically he's the biggest unlicensed fight promoter around now, especially in the capital, and that's because he's the best. He's the nicest too. He'll put himself out. You know that he's got everything covered. You can guarantee he's got a doctor and a paramedic there – he doesn't take any short cuts. He looks after his people. That's all you can ask for, really. So basically when I fight for Alan, all I've got to worry about is winning the fight. He can match me up, I'll take the fight and from then on it's fun and games. He's a top bloke, Alan – a top bloke.'

At 26 years old, Chrissy's had over 60 fights and out of them he's won 50. He's had five draws and five defeats. It's a good record but what does he put his success down to? Well, first of all, he claims he never fights anyone he thinks he can't beat! And then there's the training – of which Chrissy's not a big fan.

'I don't like to train, I'm not a good trainer. I don't train as much as a lot of people, and I don't do as much as I should. But having said that, you know, I keep myself fit and sharp – but I can't be arsed with all this roadwork stuff, it just don't suit me. I believe that I'm a natural fighter and basically, I'll always be fit for a fight. There's better things to do than training, as you get that little bit older you soon find that out. Once your experience kicks in and you start sort of learning how to see a fight through without relying on fitness, it all works out. I got my nickname, The Martini Kid, 'cos I'll travel anywhere, at anytime, for anyone, you know? I'll take fights at short notice. I've got a good chin, I've never actually been stopped, so I make for a good fight. I love a brawl and I can box a little bit. People see me in the gym and say that I'm a box puncher, that I can move, that I've got skill. But when I fight I just walk forward and hopefully please the crowd. I shouldn't really say this, it's sacrilege, but no one here really wants to see two fighters that are jabbing and not really fighting, just boxing each other. In my experience, people want to see two Mike Tysons – and that suits me down to the ground 'cos I love a brawl. That's why me and Gary Shaw will be a good fight, 'cos I think he's got the same sort of mindset as me. We're just down there punching each other 'til one of us ain't there no more.'

Chrissy's family is right behind him, supporting him all the way – even though his mum would rather he didn't fight.

'Well, I was a little scrapper at school. My mum loves me to bits and I love her. But she worries about me. She's the only person on the planet who'd say I'm too good looking to be a boxer. My old man . . . well, he doesn't show it a lot but I think he's quietly proud of me. I hear that he talks about me in the pub a little bit, but he'll never say it to my face. That's just what they do, isn't it? I've got a good family around me, and they know that they're never going to stop me doing it! My mum keeps on saying to me, "Is this your last one?" But I don't think it ever will be. I'll be fighting when I'm 60 years old, probably – well I'll try to anyway, if I live that long.'

Chrissy's family aren't the only fans in the audience – he sells his own tickets before a fight and he's guaranteed to pull a crowd.

Chrissy says: 'If you sold a ticket to everyone that promised to come and watch you'd do well on tickets! If you get a thousand people who say they'll come and watch, you'll be looking at a hundred actually coming – usually there are last-minute pull-outs and stuff like that. But I do get a lot of people coming down. Because I've been fighting at Epping for quite a few years now I pretty well know everyone in there, so there'll be quite a crowd.'

With fighters selling their own tickets, you'd think that there might be a lot of tension in the crowd between the fighters' camps, but Chrissy claims that's not the case.

'People have got an idea that with unlicensed boxing the crowd will be full of thugs, which couldn't be further from the truth. You've got nice people there. If you went to a football match you can pretty much guarantee that everyone watching has played football at some time in their lives, or at least got a very big interest in it, and that's the same with boxing. What you find though, is that if there is any trouble it's not boxers that go out and cause it on the streets outside or in the crowds, 'cos they're respectful people. Boxing teaches you a discipline, it teaches you respect. It's generally a very good atmosphere. All I can say is if you've never been to an unlicensed show, come down. Have a look and I guarantee you won't be disappointed. It's a good atmosphere.'

Another added bonus is the women – fighters do tend to get noticed.

'They notice my little flat nose, which I've broken nine times. Most people can guess that I've had a bit of a box in my time. Yeah, I suppose girls like to know you can look after yourself. I don't get boxing groupies though. I'm too ugly. I look like I've been set on fire and then put out with a paddle – so I don't get groupies. The ring girls always give you a nice smile, but I suppose that's what they're there for! In my experience ladies like to feel protected though. They like to know you can look after yourself and them, so in a way that might be attractive. I often get little notes from girls.'

Chrissy was now grinning from ear to ear, but as time was

drawing on and his fight with Gary Shaw was fast approaching I turned the conversation back to tonight's fight. Chrissy had already fought Gary once before. Chrissy had won 'on cuts', but he wasn't happy about it.

'No fighter likes to win a fight on cuts. Last time I won on cuts in the second round against Gary. You'd rather you get a decision that's a good one, or you get a stoppage, you know? But a win on cuts leaves it a bit open. You think, if I hadn't got the cut, how would the fight have gone? Personally, I do think I was winning that previous fight actually, but I think I'll beat him in this one – I wouldn't have taken it on otherwise. He's a good fighter though. He'll stand with you all day long. He's a brawler, just like myself, he's got a good chin and a good dig on him as well. He's brave and he's a skilled man – a good all-round package of fighter. But I won't take a step backwards either. I'll be there all day and we'll knock lumps off each other, everyone will love it. It'll be a good fight.'

Downstairs, approaching the ring, Gary Shaw knew exactly what he was there for. As he was announced and he stepped into the ring he looked fit and sharp and a lot like his father Roy – smaller and less pumped-up but the face was definitely Roy's. He looked a little nervous but that was to be expected. He had something to prove this time.

Steve Holdsworth announced Chrissy.

'His opponent – boxing out of the red corner – ladies and gentlemen . . . debonaire, handsome and tall – Gary's opponent is none of these! *Chrissy Morris!*'

Chrissy's shaven head came bobbing into the ring, he raised his hand and then made straight over to Gary to shake his hand. Chrissy looked very relaxed and seemed to be enjoying every minute of it. He shook everyone's hand – Gary Bedford the referee, Steve Holdsworth, Gary Shaw's corner-man – he even managed a joke with someone in the crowd. There was none of the tension or fear that seemed to come with some of his other fights. Chrissy genuinely looked like he was loving every minute of it. He was actually looking forward to the fight, it was not him being flash or showing off; it seemed that this was the place Chrissy liked to be – in the middle of a boxing ring amongst his friends with the prospect of a good, hard, fair fight ahead.

While Chrissy talked and laughed with everyone Gary paced around nervously, loosening the tension in his arms and legs. Chrissy was so laid back that he hadn't even got his gloves on yet. There was a short delay while his second laced them up.

Gary Bedford called the fighters to the centre of the ring and asked for a clean fight, and told them to break when they were told. They touched gloves and just before they went back to their corners to await the start, Chrissy leant forward and said, 'Drinks after, Gary, whatever happens, all right?' Gary nodded and they went back to their respective corners, two gentlemen fighters about to do battle – old values in young bodies.

From the bell they came out to a storming start. Chrissy held the classic boxer's stance, chin tucked into his chest, looking up through his eyebrows, elbows in and hands high. Gary was more open, elbows high, head exposed. They looked the same size and weight but so far Chrissy looked more technically sound than Gary.

At the start it was Gary who went for a quick knockout. He blazed in with four left and right hooks to the head and two uppercuts. It stunned Chrissy for a split second but, realising that he was not hurt, he came back with his own straight left jab that instantly drew blood that splattered the VIP's ringside. As Chrissy pushed forward, Gary floundered. He had no room to swing any big shots. They fell into a clinch and while Chrissy kept his head down and worked two ripping uppercuts onto Gary's chin, Gary tried to push him off. Blood was now coming from Gary's mouth and nose. Still Chrissy hit home with one more uppercut that threw Gary's head back at an acute angle. But instead of covering up or moving out of the way he stayed in the line of fire and nodded approval to Chrissy for landing a good shot. Unfortunately Chrissy did not see this gesture and whacked in another one.

The referee stepped in to separate them and inspected the damage to Gary's face. Gary said he was all right so they touched gloves and the war started again. This time Gary swung his left hand out too long and Chrissy slipped inside Gary's guard. He was devastating, keeping his punches short and crisp, aimed at Gary's nose.

But there was a steel to Gary that could not be broken. He fought back with his own left-right-left combination of short hooks. They both backed off and took deep breaths. Gary was the first to come back in. He sent out a left jab which fell short of its target. Chrissy caught it for a moment and then let it go. Gary was winding up his right hand like a windmill, but Chrissy saw it coming and his timing was perfect. He waited for the punch to come, set himself, and just leaned backwards. The punch missed, but its momentum threw Gary off balance. He stumbled forward towards the corner and Chrissy followed him. When Gary turned around to see where Chrissy was, he was smacked full on the face with a right cross that took everyone's breath away – especially Gary's. But still he remained standing. He moved back to the centre of the ring and again Chrissy came in close, doing damage with short punches to Gary's head and body. All Gary could do was push Chrissy away. Suddenly, though, Gary hit back with his own combination of uppercuts. The two fighters traded punches, pushed and wrestled each other, clashed heads and then broke to recover. They punched as they back-pedalled and then in they went again. Blood was spread across Gary's face. He soaked up Chrissy's attacks and countered with his own. When the bell finally rang for the end of the round it was to the relief of the crowd and the fighters.

When the bell sounded again, it started as it had finished, no dancing around or probing, just straight in. This time though, Gary seemed to be getting the upper hand. He followed up his left-hand straight jab with a right jab which stopped Chrissy from getting close where he was more comfortable. Chrissy wasn't being hurt but Gary was scoring more points. He pushed forward, holding Chrissy at bay and scoring some good shots.

Chrissy's corner shouted and screamed at him to get back into the fight. Gary was growing in confidence; he began sticking out his left hand, pushing Chrissy away. It seemed as though he was saying, 'You just stay there – I don't want you to come any closer.' Then he simply pulled the trigger. His shoulders twisted and his right hand came over. It smashed through Chrissy's guard and hit him on the cheek. It was a beautifully balanced shot. It stung Chrissy back into action. He took two more hooks as he came in closer to Gary and then began to work – uppercuts, hooks, little stabs – they weren't fast but they were hard. Every one got through. Every one must have hurt. They were back at each other again now, pushing, shoving, punching in that small, confined space, each fighter trying to find a little room to swing a punch, but every time getting caught with one themselves. Finally the bell went for the end of round two.

Round three seemed to come round quickly. After touching gloves, both fighters slammed into each other. Gary seemed now to have forgotten the strategy that had worked so well in the previous round. He was in there now using every ounce of strength to keep punching. Both men had taken some very hard shots and had survived. Both men had given everything. Neither man was looking a comfortable winner. You could not separate them. The round was in its last minute when a shift in the balance of the fight startled us.

Gary threw a right jab and Chrissy just seemed to bend his knees slightly and bowed down at the same time. Gary's jab missed and Chrissy saw in front of him an open, unguarded target. He let fly with a perfectly timed left uppercut and a right hook – fast and hard. The result shook Gary to the core. Suddenly the advantage shifted properly towards Chrissy. He was back in control, the move had given him a boost of confidence and energy. Gary was now on the back foot. He was defending and not attacking. Everything he did was reacting to Chrissy's moves and when the final bell went Gary looked beaten.

The result went to Chrissy Morris, but it was close. The referee almost announced it a draw but scored it 29–28 in Chrissy's favour. After handshakes all round the fighters left the ring. Alan was pleased with the fight but he looked tense. He had every right to be. Next up was his son, Jamie.

EIGHT

JAMIE HAS BEEN GOING TO FIGHTS THAT HIS DAD HAS ORGANISED since he was a toddler, but he'd always been in the audience, never in the ring – until now. He told me: 'I always enjoyed it, always fancied getting in there but I'd not quite had the incentive, so I never did. Then I got the phone call from my dad a couple of weeks ago just offering me a fight and an opportunity to train with him. So I took him up on it and that was that – I haven't looked back since. I've been training every day at the Peacock Gym in Canning Town, weightlifting up at the Country Club, doing lots of running – three- and five-mile runs – all sorts of fitness and boxing exercises. I got right into it and I'm looking forward to the fight.'

Alan is his trainer too. And he's certainly not soft on him because he's his son.

'Dad's a very good trainer. When we get in the gym he's just totally different – I don't really see him as my dad when we're there. He trains me very, very hard, gets me running on the machines. He really pushes me. After a mile I'm tired and then I'll do another mile. When I'm sparring and I can't go on any more, he pushes me that extra bit which gives me the real power to go on. The ground work is very hard. He just helps me get initiative which I think I need, to do that extra little bit more than the person I'm fighting.

'Sometimes it's so hard that I just want to stop. But at the end of the day you're going in there to have a fight. I mean you can't just give up and walk away – that's no good when you're going in to have a fight. You've got to train harder than the person you're fighting otherwise it isn't worth getting into the ring. You've got to be 100 per cent seriously involved in it all the time.

'The guy I'm fighting goes by the name of Liam The Kid. He's 29 years old and he's a novice. Like me, he's not had any fights, so we're pretty evenly matched. Otherwise, I don't know much about him. I've heard he's got potential and he's game for a fight. We'll see how it goes, you know?

'I've always been into it, seeing as my dad's been into it most of his life, training fighters. I've just grown up naturally around it. I was always on the pads, popping down the gym, training here and there. But I've never been seriously trained for a fight like I am now. Recently we've been going down the gym in Canning Town, sparring with some travellers down there, like a young boy called Mike, who's 20 years old, a very hard fighter, you could carry on hitting him all day long and then he'll still stay standing – so that's good experience for me.

'You need a lot of heart, a lot of commitment and a lot of time as well to do this. You've got to be prepared to get down to that gym after work, and do another hard day's work in the gym. You've got to be prepared to take a punch and get in the ring and spar with hard people and go four or five rounds with them. It's not an easy game but it's very enjoyable.

'I'm feeling very confident today, to be honest. It's not bothered me as much you might think. I train where the actual show's going to be held, so when I go through to the gym I walk down the walkway, where you actually walk towards the fight. I get nervous sometimes when I'm walking through there because I can imagine the people, the music – all the good buzz. So I'm looking forward to it. I'm not that nervous at the moment.

'All my friends are coming down to see me fight – a lot of people from work, including my boss – so even if that doesn't really pressurise you, it's in the back of your mind. You know they're there and it makes you want to go out and win for them.

'Before a fight my dad's just going at it non-stop. When we're down the gym, everyone there is all over him – he's got people coming up to him about tickets, people wanting to take him on the pads, the phone is ringing constantly all day long. It's hard work for him, to train me – you've got to give him respect for all he does for me.

'I'm gonna win this fight. Afterwards I would like to carry on – we'll see how it goes and if I enjoy it I'll carry on the training and hopefully get prepared for the next show. I'll take it from there, but this training has done me a lot of good.

'My mum's not very happy about me fighting. I can understand where she's coming from – it must be a big worry for her, having her son getting punched in a boxing ring. But I know they're good shows, and there are good doctors around. If I thought there was any real danger in it at all then I wouldn't be getting in there. I've got two kids of my own, after all.

'When I started training for this fight I was like any other guy really, going out clubbing, raving, smoking 15 fags a day maybe, having the odd spliff, things like that, you know? But training has just given me that extra something to stop all that. Without the training I wouldn't have been able to stop smoking, stop cannabis, or stop going out – because there was nothing else there for me. Now I come home from work and I look forward to going training instead of just sitting down in front of the television to watch *Eastenders*, with a fag and a can of beer. I come home from work, have a bath, then go down the gym. It's given me something to get into.

'I want to win very badly today. I've got a lot to prove in there. I've not done all this training for nothing, so I'm going in there to win, nothing else. I feel very confident.'

Jamie's father, Alan, never forced his children to get into fighting but he never discouraged them either. He says: 'I'll put you in the picture. I've got four sons and all of them, apart from the youngest who's 15, have fought and I've trained 'em all. In a way they started training when they were six years old. I used to teach 'em to fight in the garden. I taught them never to be bullies – none of them have ever been bullies – but they can all look after themselves. They all fought from a very young age in the ring. Jamie is 22 now, the last time he fought was when he was 12, as an amatuer. He used to be a kick boxer and he would win. But over the last few months he really wanted to fight unlicensed. His brother Sean fought unlicensed boxing when he was 16. He was the youngest prize fighter in those days. He did well too – he had two fights and won them both by knockouts. He was a very strong fighter and Jamie wants to get in there now and do the same.

'When Sean was fighting once, I was sitting next to the doctor at a ringside table, and I was half out of my seat. The doctor had a hold of my hand, feeling my pulse – so you can imagine I was screaming and shouting for him. You don't want to see them hurt, obviously, but if you train them right . . . it's not nice but it's not too nasty. I suppose if you asked his mum it would be different! She don't like him fighting at all, you know? But I know they've done the work in the gym and they're matched properly, so it's up to them. It's their choice – if they don't want to fight there's no way I'll make them. I'm not one of those that want to just push 'em in there.

'He's a parent now. He's only 22 but we've got a little granddaughter now, and to be quite honest with you I think he was a little bit aimless before he started training. Obviously, he was looking after his family but I don't think he really had a goal in life. He was just going from one job to the other. And then when this opportunity came up, it was only by chance I said, "Do you want to get on the bill?" and he said he did. I've seen a brilliant change in him, to be truthful. He hasn't stopped training. I mean we're in the third week of training. He was on 15 fags a day and he stopped completely – which is great, just to be able to do that. He used to have the odd bit of a draw too, like youngsters do – you know, nothing major but I think it was a problem. I think it slows 'em up, you know what I mean? Makes 'em a bit laid back and it affects their work. But he's knocked that right on the nut. I've noticed how bright and together he is out there. So what with that and the drinking (although he was never really a great drinker, but he liked the odd pint), which he knocked on the nut for the fight, that's a great change, I think, in anybody's life. He's a different person. He's got a brightness about him and he hasn't stopped training. In three weeks he's had just two days off with a bit of flu.

'It goes back to the days of old when people were fighting one another and the strongest survived. The crowd would always gather round to see, just like the school playground. I think it's inbuilt in men, that it's just part and parcel of that animal instinct that goes all the way back. The events that we do, I wouldn't class them as violent. They're controlled boxing tournaments – it all depends on what you see as violent. A street fight is violent; somebody being hit with an iron bar is violent – but what we do I don't believe is violence. It's a sport. It all depends on your attitude, I think.

'It often involves the same reaction people have when they stop and look at an accident, when they see the police and the ambulance and a crowd gathers – I suppose it's morbid curiosity we're talking about. I think a lot of people wish that they were actually in there in the ring too. It's inbuilt in them, there's always a bit of fighter in people. Maybe they haven't ever trained – they don't want to get hurt – but they do want to see two guys in there doing it. The crowd likes to see the knockout. So in all forms of fighting sports, if people were truthful about it, the thrill does stem back to when they were young and in the school playground two kids went at it, in front of a great big crowd.

'I reckon it's a very stress-filled society these days and a lot of my fighters, believe it or not, are in high-powered jobs: they've got their own companies, or they're stockbrokers, say, and they find it's a good stress release. So possibly they let that pent-up aggression out during the training – and the ultimate way to let it out is to have three rounds at one of our events.

'Practically anybody can take part that's fit in a boxing environment. The WPA's not just boxing, it's kick boxing also. If you want to get anywhere in the pro game you've got to give up work. You need a sponsor and you have to train every day of the week. So there's guys out there who don't want to be pro boxers but they want to box, so the WPA is in the middle – it's in between the amateur and the professional. We offer something for all those people that may have the stressful jobs. I've got stockbrokers who are on the market floor at 6.30 in the morning coming to train with me at night and taking part in events. They find that it's their way of releasing their energies, you know? They'll never become pro boxers and they don't want to become pro boxers – so that's where we step in, with what we do. We get ordinary boxers and amateur boxers who want to come and fight for us and we get pro boxers that have given up the pro game because they haven't got anywhere. But they got somewhere with us. We get ex-professional fighters who, at 30 years old, are considered washed-up in professional boxing but who are still fit, strong men. They come and fight for us, too. So we open up a vast opportunity to people who want to take part in our type of sport.

'Before the kind of event that's coming up here, we just did our own thing. If kick boxing was part of the show we were sanctioned by kick boxing organisations. It's got to the point now that there's such an interest in the type of boxing that we do that we see that the way forward is to actually licence the boxers – and the way that we're going to do that is much the same, if you like, as the way the Boxing Board of Control do it. Our boxers will go to their doctor with a form, have a full medical to show that they're fit, have an optician's test to make sure that their eyes are fine and then they will come back to us with the results so that we know that everything's kosher and above board and that they're fit to fight. They'll be issued with a WPA licence and a record book. Every event that they fight in, win, lose or draw, will be entered in the licence records and then that way we know exactly where they've been, what they've done, who they've fought and how they've won or lost their bout.

'I've been at events with fighters – my own fighters – where the boxing-ring ropes were slack and you'd tell the event organiser about it and nothing was done. I remember a particular incident years ago when one of the boys fell out of the ring straight onto the concrete floor and smashed his head. I was the first one over to him and I shouted out to the promoter, "Get the doctor over." The guy didn't have a doctor there. I really remonstrated and pulled the promoter up and then we pulled all our fighters out and left.

'The WPA is also a sanctioning body. There's promoters up and down the country who want to be sanctioned by us, which means that when they ask the WPA to sanction the event they will take our doctors, our paramedics, our ambulances on board. Every event will have to be covered and sanctioned in that way to cut out the cowboys. But there's not that many promoters in the country, we've probably got about five or six promoters at the moment that will be coming under the banner.

'If you read the history books, before the Boxing Board came into power there was bare-knuckle boxing. Guys were out in the field fighting each other. Then they brought the one-rope ring in and then they started to bring in the whips and the corners. So anyway, that was the forerunner, the first type of boxing. So then came the Queensbury rules and then eventually you got the Boxing Board of Control. That's how it evolved. What we're doing is in between amateur and professional.

'The boys love it, it's their sport. You've got people who are into rugby football or show-jumping, or golf as a hobby. This is what these guys' hobby is because they haven't got the time to be a professional boxer. So the aim of the organisation now is regulation. We're getting so many people that want to take part, so many people that want to box in these events, we are having to regulate it. I don't want to say we'll become a Boxing Board of Control, because I hate the word "control" – but we're going to be an association and we'll move forward, and do our licensing.

'I work between a group of different promoters and I get right stuck into helping them get the fights matched and the events organised. I work for the Epping Forest Country Club as their sports coordinator. Anybody that wants to come and put on a sporting event there comes pretty much through me – and most of it is boxing or kick boxing. So I am the hands-on troubleshooter between the promoter, the Country Club and the fighters. On top of that I've got a stable of six or seven of my own fighters who all take part in these shows. So I'm also getting boys ready for the fights. I founded the WPA (World Prize Ring Association) and now I need people around me. I've got a very good guy called Steve Kerridge who handles the kick boxing side of WPA.

'It's non-stop once you get involved in it. You might work with some promoters who don't even know how to put a poster together so you'll sometimes have to help them design the poster, and then it's constant telephone calls. First of all you might have to ring round if you're matchmaking and then you'll be dealing with the trainers and with the fighters themselves and you'll be working with both sets. They'll ask about what their opponent's capable of, his size, weight, or his knockout record. I myself will tell it as it is – I'll say if the guy's a bit bigger, or if he's not a banger or if he's got a knockout or if he has got a big punch on him. You really have to be honest with people. The one thing I won't do is moody 'em up and say they've got an easy fight when they haven't. I have my reputation to think of.

'And then you've got the security to organise. We carry big security at our events at the Country Club. You could go to some events and unfortunately you know they don't carry anything. We carry about 14 security men and there's security meetings to make sure everything's running smoothly. We have to plan the CCTV – 19 cameras in all, everything like that to sort out. We deal with the managers in the Country Club. They set out the chairs but we deal with the ring man and make sure he's not late. You'll ring him two, three, maybe four times – he probably thinks you're mad, making sure that he's got the date booked okay. That's one of the main worries – if the ring itself didn't turn up! You're worrying whether the fighters are going to turn up or whether they're gonna be late.

'Okay, so when we're organising an event or when I'm organising a promotion I will start initial approaches to the fighters to get the groundwork and the running order. I'll sit down first of all and I'll write down a fight – who I think would be the good choice for a good fight. Then once I've got that done I'll ring everybody up and see if they're available – usually they are. Then, once we've laid down who's going to be fighting, I'll ask the fighters to send photographs through of themselves. Then we'll sit down and design a poster, unless it's been designed already, but usually they leave it to us. Next, I'll get a rough draft for the poster which I'll then give to my son and he'll put it together more. Then we go to the designer and we sit there with him at the computer until we've pulled the poster together properly, 'cos the poster is very, very important to bring the crowd in – and for the fighters too, they love it. I've got to be honest with you, they make every fighter that's on the poster look like a world champion! From here on, it's obviously a case of booking the ring, the doctor, the paramedic. If you've got championship fights you've got to order the championship belt for the different weight divisions that are fighting. Soon you're dealing with the printer for the posters, tickets, fliers, etc, which then get given over to the promoters who distribute them amongst the people right up to about a month before the event. Then the advertising campaign will start. Posters will go up in the streets, shops, pubs, clubs, bookmakers, all over the different areas. A couple of thousand posters will go up and fliers will go out. There'll be interviews, press releases to newspapers, that type of thing. And, of course, you're always on the phone talking to the fighters themselves right the way through. Sometimes you have to coax them right through until the fight.

'Fighters can sometimes get injured. I've had guys ring up the day of a major fight with the flu. We've got a fighter called Hughie Robinson, he doesn't fight for us any more, but one time he was defending his British unlicensed title and he had close on 300 people coming to watch him. He was fighting a guy called Tony Louis, and I was monitoring the situation leading up to the fight. The fight was on

NATURAL BORN FIGHTERS

91

the Sunday and on the Wednesday I rung Tony Louis and I said, "Are you all right?" and he said, "Yeah, I'm out in Yorkshire running up and down mountains, I'm as fit as a fiddle." On the Saturday morning, the day before the event, he rang and spoke to my son. Sean then came to me – I remember it, he was standing at the bottom of the stairs, face as long as a kite – I didn't know what had happened. And he said, "Dad, I've got some bad news for you." I said, "What?" and he said, "Tony Louis's got the flu, he can't fight." That just threw everything for that day.

'So I rung Tony up and said, "Tony, you've got to fight, we need you there, never mind the flu." He was coughing and spluttering – but he got there and he fought, you know? But it was nearly a disaster: we couldn't get anybody to come in at that short notice to fight.'

Alan continues: 'You've got a lot of the fighters that won't let you down, they're solid. For example, you've got Roland the Russian, you've got The Essex Terminator – Paul Kavanagh, Tiger, guys like that. There's Gary Shaw, Chrissy Morris too. They won't let you down. You know that you can count on them. Their arms would have to be falling off before they let you down. You do get guys on the fringes who sometimes do get the flu, or get injured in sparring. I've had boys get cut a week or two before a fight. But that's what the game's about. And that's why, when you're matching you match more fights than the number you're really going to put on eventually. Sometimes you will get the full contingent – I've put 14 fighters on in a night – and sometimes you might get 8, it all depends how the shows go.

'I get very tense sometimes. I think I'm perfectly all right, but my wife doesn't. She says I go from being hyperactive to just sitting and staring. I'll try and describe it: if you imagine 500 thoughts going on in your mind and you're trying and get them into order and it's constantly on at you for about a month before the fight. Then three weeks away it starts getting a bit worse, and by two weeks away it's just constant – that's all you think about. You go to bed at night and you'll think of something so you have to get up and write it down. That's what its like. Although for this event I'm sleeping all right as it happens. I can still feel my stomach turning over, though. But then that's my job for you!

'Yesterday I was in the gymnasium and it's funny – I've noticed this lately – when people know that you're involved in unlicensed fighting, they kinda think there's a mystique, a mysterious aura to what we do. I went into the changing-room yesterday and a guy goes, "Do you have security at these events?" I went, "Well, of course we do." They think that something bad's going to happen like in the old days. And if they do come they realise that it's as good as – if not better than – professional shows. The way things are run and organised is better. The fights are more exciting. I've been in the pro game, I've trained pro fighters and our game really is more exciting. Not all the time admittedly, I mean you get good, evenly matched pro fights and championship fights; a lot of good friends of mine are pro boxers and trainers – it's great. But the majority of our fights are good and exciting because the boys have a tear-up and they only fight for three twos. We are now going into championships and they are so evenly matched that there's no mismatches. You see a real fight, a real toe-to-toe battle.

'I think possibly the general public don't really know what we do. They think our fighting is bare-knuckle fighting out in a field somewhere or in a warehouse. Some of the films that have come out lately portray it like that. They think that you get two guys, probably with no gloves on, head-butting and elbowing, maybe biting and kicking each other to bits and that doesn't happen. It's nothing like that at all. That's what the public think, but they're getting re-educated. Besides, at the shows now we're getting a cross-section of people coming, perhaps guys might come with their wives and their girlfriends. In the old days it was pretty much a man's job, going to the unlicensed boxing. But it's different now.

'I think it's better, more exciting to us because the guys aren't pro boxers, they're guys that hold down ordinary types of jobs and so they aren't training solidly like a pro does every day. But in many ways there's not a huge difference between our fights and the pro fights.

The rules are often the same, although we only fight for two-minute rounds and the pros fight for three minutes. We do three two-minute rounds, six two-minute rounds and if we're doing a big world title fight we'll bring in three-minute rounds 'cos it suits the fighters. But the majority are two minutes. But our medical supervision is exactly the same. We have ringside doctors, two paramedics with the full oxygen resuscitation unit at the ringside, with a stretcher obviously, and a fully equipped ambulance outside the arena. The local hospital is notified that there's a fight going on by the paramedics so they're ready if – God forbid – anything occurred. The fighters would be rushed straight down there by ambulance. Our referee is a qualified referee, the gloves are the same weight and size as the ones professional boxers use – no difference.'

NINE

ALAN EXPLAINS THE LINE-UP AHEAD FOR THE WPA. 'AT THE TOP of the bill we've got Decca (Derek) Simpkin. I call him the Northern Giant. He's 19½st and 6ft 6ins. He's an ex-professional fighter from Birmingham. Decca's had about 45 pro fights I believe, and he's won probably about half of them. Decca's 44 years old and he's fitter than a lot of the young guys that I know, so people out there who say he's over the hill wouldn't be able to go the distance with the man. He's fighting an American we're bringing in called Mike Middleton. He's got a good record, Mike. He started boxing during Operation Desert Storm in the American army, I believe. He's between 15½ and 16st and these guys will be fighting for the first WPA world championship. The way that I match a fight is by looking at the men's ability and their weight first of all. Our last promotion, for instance, matched Roland the Russian – a 16st heavyweight from Lithuania who trains out of Canning Town at the moment – and Shane Stanton. The Russian's had 30 fights, Stanton's had about 11 boxing bouts and about 15 or 16 kick boxing bouts, so we're looking at an even par for both men.

'In this fight, Simpkin, apart from being one of the biggest, heaviest guys about, has a way of fighting that's straightforward. He likes a tear-up. He was a pro boxer but he doesn't take a backwards step. I've never seen Middleton fight but I've heard that he also has fought some very, very tough pro fights in the States. You're gonna see a real battle between these two guys. From what I've heard, Middleton's kind of a defensive fighter who's good for about three or four rounds and then he tends to peter out. And knowing Decca Simpkins he will just go straight at him, he'll go for the big knockout. It'll be very exciting.

'Obviously I'd like to see the Englishman take it but it'll be down to the judges and the referee. Simpkin's got the weight advantage, he's 3st heavier. I think he could do the job. But I spoke to Mike Middleton on the phone and he's coming to win. He said, "I'm gonna be taking that belt back to Florida." He's training with some good people; he's sparring with Mike Tyson's sparring partner. He doesn't mess about, this guy. He's got a good record and he's got a job to do.

'There's also fear involved in these shows about what can happen. And some of the major fears going on in the back of a promoter's mind are things like what if we had a power cut; what if something occurred and the show couldn't happen, or there was a flood. Well, over the last two promotions both of those things have occurred. On one occasion we'd arranged a fight and everybody was arriving – the promoters, the doctors, the fighters were coming in and the doors were due to open at 6 p.m. The first fight was scheduled for 7 p.m. and the DJ was there testing his equipment and I'm sitting there just generally talking with people and all of a sudden the music and the lights went off. Twenty minutes went past before somebody came up and told us there'd been a blackout, a power cut all over the area. Now just imagine – you've got people coming from all over the country! It's quite a drama. That's when you start to pray. We were told the power was due to come back on but ended up having to do the medical examinations by torchlight. Eventually, though, the lights come back on and everything was fine. Then the place got flooded a week before a fight when we had really bad weather. There was three foot of water in the venue! They're the type of things that can knock you for six.

'I'm always thrilled at one particular part of the event – when the bell rings for the first round. You can relax. The boys that do the whipping to get the fighters out do a brilliant job, they're top people. But that's the only time when you can relax. Up to then it's hard to describe the feeling that you get. The stress levels are really high, I don't know how to describe it, it's like Christmas, going to court, taking your driving test – all rolled into one.

'There's room for us alongside the Boxing Board of Control. We're not asking for help from them, nor do we want to have a go at them or anything like that but our sport is our sport and in the future I see fighters being licensed; I see promoters up and down the country promoting WPA fights, and I see it going from strength to strength. Our bills will be mixed, there'll be boxing and kick boxing. You get that in America and that's where America's in front of us. If we could have done it and worked with the Board of Control then it would have been great. But the trouble with certain people at the Board of Control is that they turn round and go, "Oh, these unlicensed boxers – their medical supervision is terrible." But I'd say that if any of the doctors want to come to any of the WPA shows they're more than welcome. They can see the medicals taking place and sit ringside but they've never been, so they criticise.

'This event is a flagship for the WPA first world championship title fight. It'll take us into a realm where we've never been before. We'll put on bigger fights, and we'll go to bigger venues. I'd like to see WPA fights down at the Royal Albert Hall, there's no reason why they shouldn't be there, or the London Arena, or Wembley, because the fights are quality, they're exciting.

'If you just go to a normal type of show, right, you've got all the lights on and it will be a 20-minute wait. It's dreary and nothing's going on. When you come to one of our events it's different. My son, Sean, who's stage-managing this event, has got us some live MC rappers and garage music that will come on in the interval. We've got a live PA and they get on there and they rap and they do their stuff. The audience go wild. Instead of them just going to the bar and having a chat you've got this going on. We've got ring girls that the *Sunday Sport* sent us and they're identical twin sisters. When the fighters come out you've got strobe lights going, you've got laser beams going . . . it drives the crowd crazy.'

In the changing-room above the Atlantis bar, Alan was taking no chances with his son's first unlicensed boxing match. In a huddle, Alan and Rod, another top trainer, began to pray with Jamie.

'I pray that he won't rush, I pray that neither man will be hurt, but I pray for victory for Jamie,' says Alan. 'Amen.'

'Amen.'

This is a local derby between two East End lads: Jamie versus Liam The Kid. It's the first of these fights for both of them and they come out with all guns blazing. In this fight there were only three one-and-a-half-minute rounds, so they couldn't afford to hang around. Liam and Jamie would be at it from bell to bell.

There was no standing back in this fight. There was no technical brilliance either – this was a tear-up. Raw and hard. Both fighters were nervous but that was natural, both had something to prove in front of families and friends and training partners. Both wanted to give everything and not look weak or not game enough. They had trained for months and gave up their normal lives to do this and their night had come.

Liam appeared with a ramrod-straight back; he did not bend at the waist or bob from the knees. He presented a static target for Jamie. But he had a hard and fast jab that could sting too. Jamie was all movement, making it difficult for Liam to hit him. When he did stop to get his own shots in he varied them from head to body in combinations of jabs and hooks. Liam held the centre of the ring and Jamie circled around him, slamming in with straight jabs and a sharp right hook to Liam's ribs. Liam was surprised and shocked by the speed and ferocity of Jamie's attack but he held his ground and let fly with shots of his own. Suddenly Jamie stopped the onslaught and seemed surprised that Liam was still standing and still in his face. He ducked down and grabbed Liam around the waist. Gary Bedford stepped in to separate them.

The frantic pace dropped slightly, both fighters relying on their jabs to keep the other at bay. Liam fired a jab which Jamie sidestepped and shot out his own. Liam countered with a left hook to the side of Jamie's head. They were matching blow for blow, both hitting hard, neither of them backing off. The round ended all-square.

They came out for round two and this time Liam led the attack as he came at Jamie with a left and a right. Jamie had seen them coming and ducked, bent his knees and slipped them, then from a low position he came back with the best flurry of punches in the fight – a left hook to the face, right hook to the body, then a straight left jab again to the face. For the first time Liam took two steps backwards and turned his back to Jamie – he was getting hurt. Jamie kept up the momentum with good, deliberate, hard punches. But as Liam's back was turned against him he landed two punches on the back of Liam's head – and in boxing that's not allowed. Gary Bedford stepped in to stop the action.

When the fight resumed, Jamie once more threw a jab and once more it hit home. He followed it with a straight right. He kept pushing forward and Liam was forced back onto the ropes. He bounced off them and threw two punches in reply, both hitting their intended target. Now it was Jamie's turn to go back into the centre of the ring and that's where they stayed in a clinch, neither one moving. The bell rang for the end of round two – another even round. An appreciative crowd applauded the two fighters.

In the corners, water was poured into the two mens' mouths and over their heads. Fresh Vaseline was spread over their eyebrows, sore cheeks and scratches. Instructions were given but they were not taken on board – the fighters were nearing the end of their reserves of strength, they knew they had to go back in there in a few seconds and neither man was relishing the idea.

In round three, Liam came out with a new determination and from the centre of the ring he came at Jamie. He took a left to the body, a jab to the head, stumbled backwards and fell against the ropes. Then a right uppercut to his chin and a right to the side of his head. Jamie could not throw his own punches but he was not covering up either. Still on the ropes, he raised his gloves and tried protecting his head, but still Liam flew in. Jamie pulled Liam in and held on until Gary Bedford separated them. Liam looked long and hard into Jamie's eyes to see if he could see any weakness, any sign that Jamie did not want to go on, but he saw nothing of the sort.

They came back to the centre of the ring and, realising that time was running out, started slogging at each other. It was punch for punch. The crowd were on their feet getting caught up in the battle, urging the fighters on. Both men refused to give in, the punches didn't get any weaker, they just kept pouring in. Every punch was an accurate one; every one landed clean.

When the bell sounded for the end of the fight they embraced each other in mutual respect. They had survived the ordeal, given a good account of themselves and no one was let down.

The decision was the right one – a draw.

The main bout of the evening was to be the heavyweight contest between Decca Simpkin from Derby and Mike Middleton from Tampa Bay, Florida.

Mike was a professional licensed fighter with a good record and a burning desire to win a title. He told me: 'I started in martial arts when I was a kid and then I played athletics in high school. In college I played football and baseball and wrestled and I then went into the army and when I was there I started boxing. Basically it was just a diversion – and I did OK but I never really tried to pursue it that much back then. After I finished my army career I started kick boxing and I did pretty well at that.

'I've had a total of nineteen fights, and lost eight or nine times. I just fought a month ago, right before Super Bowl and I won that one. I never had any money behind me. The guys who tend to be super-successful have a lot of money and they can often almost pick their opponents. I've had some good opponents but I've basically lost nearly every fight I was expected to lose (I won a few of them) and I've won every fight I should have won. Boxing's just a funny sport in the fact that in any other sport you can think of – football, baseball, polo – if you have a bad day or a bad game you can come back the next day and people have forgotten it. In boxing, if you have a bad night and you lose, you look bad and people don't forget that and you don't fight again, when it comes to professional fighters, sometimes for a year. So if you look bad – for instance like David Tua didn't look great when he fought Lennox Lewis – people will base your whole career on that one time when you just had a bad night. Tua can't just come back the next night, like Michael Jordan could, and score 70 points. Boxing is the only sport where you're only as good as that last fight.

'I try and arrange my training around my work schedule. I make my own work schedule so I'm pretty lucky in that respect. But I get up early and run. I live in a good area to run and I come home, get in the shower, eat my breakfast then *boom* off to work. I work all day. Then from work I go to the gym and I train, spar, do all my stuff and then come home. I do that three days a week and the other days of the week I go with my wife very early in the morning to lift weights with her.

'When I run I usually do between three and five miles. I try and go at a pretty good pace. I don't do it so much for maintenance of weight, more for cardiovascular endurance. When I lift weights, one day I do upper body, the next I do lower body and I just alternate those. I eat five to six times a day – small meals to keep my metabolism going. Jill, my wife, does the same thing, basically. She works out with me and does running and stuff on her own.

'The reason this fight coming up is so important is because it's a title shot. Some people fight a long time and never get a shot at the title. My buddy Alex Stewart fought Tyson, Holyfield, George Foreman, Michael Moore but he never got a go. He says it's his only regret. If I can get a shot at a title, that to me is the most important thing – to say, "I fought for a title and I have a belt." That'll make my career.

'I have a very good jab and I move well on the outside and I can bang punch. Alex says I'm the hardest hitting white kid he's ever fought with and he's sparred with a lot of people. I try to stay outside so that I can feel what kind of fight it's going to be. Once I get you hurt, that's it, I'm in. I keep going till the ref steps in or you're asleep.

'I think he's going to come out at me quickly, probably for two different reasons. One – he's older so I'm not sure if he's going to have the endurance for a long war. Two – I think it's to his benefit because it's his home town, his crowd – everything is in his favour, his adrenaline's going to be going and he'll be pumped up and ready to put on a show. I think he's going to come out and jump on me. That's what I think is going to happen. And I've just got to weather that storm for the first round and then after that I think I'll be fine.

'To me boxing's the ultimate sport. You can't depend on anybody else, you have to depend on yourself alone and I think that your personality comes out. The things that I think of when I think of boxing are dedication, drive, determination – and that's the kind of stuff I want in my other careers too, in other parts of my life.

'The training you get in the army as far as hand-to-hand combat goes is pretty minor. It's done in basic training unless you go on to other aspects of military life. If you're a tank driver or a gunner or a helicopter pilot you're not going to have to learn those things. Guys in the special forces like the SAS over here, those guys have to know that kind of stuff. That's part of your job. But to tell you the truth, boxing for me initially was a way to get out of duty in the afternoons. I used to get off work early.

'There are people who wonder how Mike Tyson would be in a street fight. You don't know because a street fight lasts usually 15 maybe 20 seconds and then somebody's done – a street fight's so different. I mean I haven't done it, I can't remember the last time I got into a fight. You know, I would probably be at a disadvantage because I would be thinking about the Marquess of Queensbury rules – don't hit him low – while the other guy's probably trying to kick my knee out or hit me with a chair. I think that Derek's style will be aggressive in there but I guess there's still going to be rules, so I'm not too worried about anything like that happening.

'My wife doesn't care for it too much. We've been together since high school. When I fought in New York a couple of fights ago, she said it was the best one I ever had because she didn't have to go! She didn't have to stand there and watch and have people going: "Are you OK? Is everything OK?" I say to her, "It can't be that bad, it's like watching me doing any other sport," (she's seen me playing sports my whole life). And she says, "It's nothing compared to everything else – how would you feel if you saw somebody hit me in the face and punch me until I was stumbling around? It's totally different." She doesn't care for it in that respect.

'She comes to my fights when they're local and she can get to them. The best thing about my wife, though, as far as my fights are concerned, is that she doesn't judge my performance. In my mind I know she cares if I win or lose but I know she's more concerned that I'm OK.

'I'm starting to get to the point now where I'm starting to feel aches and pains in my shoulders and my hands. I'm constantly complaining. My hands have been broken numerous times. My nose has been broken a couple of times too. I can't breathe through it like I should. It's all crooked now, whereas it used to be nice and straight. It's all messed up. So I think I'll know when it's time to quit. I'm also smart enough to know I don't have to do this. It's not that I have to do this to make money, like a lot of fighters who have to fight 'cos they can't do anything else. I'm lucky, I can do other things.

'I'm really looking forward to the fight. I'm trying to focus on that. But I'm also looking forward to being here and meeting the British. We have a lot of British tourists coming to Florida all the time. They're nice people, very polite and very open. I'm looking forward to being in this culture and atmosphere. The only thing I worry about, the only thing I can ever remember seeing bad about Britain, is the soccer fans, those hooligans – those guys were nuts, but other than that, I'm looking forward to being here.'

Mike has had experience of his fights being filmed. He says: 'The interesting thing about televised fights is that it's not as glamorous as it looks. When you're watching on TV, the press conferences and all that stuff looks great but it's all a pain in the butt. It's all work. It's funny how people think, "Well, he's making so much money, what does it matter?" It's actually not a lot of money at my level. Still, it's work, and it's fun seeing how things go on behind the scenes. There's what's called a "swing bout", for example. It's where they have three scheduled bouts, but if one of those ends quickly 'cos of knockout or something like that, they have a swing bout where someone steps in and fights for TV. So in a swing bout, say, in the second round it looks like one guy's going to get knocked out so they say to you, "Quick, get ready, this guy's going out, you got to come up, you're next." Well, he doesn't get knocked out then, so you sit back down and you wait until they come back and say, "OK get ready." And this goes on all night. That's just the worst because you're ready, then they're not ready, and you try and get focused and then you have to sit down.

'Lots of times, as far a being televised goes, a lot of it's luck. The times I've been televised I was not the guy they were really televising, the other dude was. I was the guy that that guy was fighting. I've never been the one that had the people behind him – whose manager and trainer with money behind him go, "We've got a really tough kid coming up. We want to put him on a ESPN or Fox." But that's where you start out if you have money behind you. They can say, "Hey, I got a kid and I'll fly him out if you put him on the show." There's a lot of wrangling and dealings that goes on behind the scenes in boxing, it's a lot of, "You wash my back, I'll wash yours; if you put my kid on this month, I'll put two of your guys on next month."

'I'm pretty happy with my life the way it's been, I've been pretty lucky and I think I'm proudest because I never got anything from anybody. My father died when I was young, my family didn't have the money to put me through school so everything I did I got on my own.

But that is the American dream to me. Nowadays I'm not rich but I'm doing OK and I've got a great wife, the love of my life, and we're going to have kids soon. I feel like I'm living the American dream.'

Mike has a message for Decca: 'I'm coming after you and I'm going to be there all night long. You can throw everything you've got at me and I'll be still in front of you. I guarantee I'll win by attrition.' He tells me: 'I won't go out and knock him out in one round, two rounds or three rounds, but in the seventh, eighth, ninth and tenth rounds – that's when I'm going to start turning on.'

The man that Mike was due to be fighting was Derek 'Decca' Simpkin. He tells me: 'I've been training really hard for this fight and it's a ten rounder and I get better towards the end. After four or five rounds I'll come into my own, I'll take his head off, I'll just punch him silly. Obviously I'm, like, 19st and I'm a shade slower than the normal person but after three or four rounds they start getting slower too and I come into my own because I'm stronger and I've got a lot of stamina. I keep going on like you wouldn't believe and I start knocking them about. Then that's it – I finish them off. I'll be on him, on him, on him; punch the crap out from him. I'll be on top of him.' Decca is 44 years old, 6ft tall, weighs 19st and has been a fighter all his life. The walls of his home are covered with photographs of him fighting. I visited him there to interview him. He told me: 'I left school and like everybody else there I went on a building site and did a normal job. I didn't fancy doing that for the rest of my life though so I went into fighting. I did a bit of bouncing, a bit of debt collecting, things like that too. That suited my character more than going to work every day, seven days a week. The violent side might not suit most people, but I got better and better at it, so I've made a good living out of violence.

'You do something like beat somebody up and by the time it's gone round Derby or wherever it's got that big that people are saying you've killed someone and buried them. It gets out of control, a reputation. I've been bouncing for 30 years, see, so after 30 years of knocking people about I've got one hell of a reputation 'cos you've knocked a hell of a lot of people about.

'But this fight means a lot to me. It's a world title fight and anything with a world title belt is an achievement. I'd be the best fighter in the world at WPA, the best fighter at that kind of fighting. Obviously I'm training for it, doing extra running. I run with my three lads, who are all professional boxers. We run three miles early in the morning, and I go over to Birmingham to their gym and I spar with them twice a week and then I hit the heavy bag out the back here. I do weightlifting too, so I'm really strong as well. I keep my weight at 19st and I fight well on it. Some people think it's a bit heavy but it suits me.'

Vikki, Decca's wife, is a small, pretty woman who at the time of the fight was pregnant. I wondered how she felt about his lifestyle, but according to Decca it was no problem.

'My wife is used to it,' he says. 'I've been fighting since she met me and I've been bouncing, all the time too, so it's an ongoing thing – it's part of me. Without violence I wouldn't be Decca Simpkin.

'After 30 years bouncing I've got quite a few stories. Some of the most frightening involve bike gangs – you see, if you get one gang of about 30, 40 lads and they fall out with another gang and they both come into the club at the same time, you got a situation. You've got to keep them apart, that's the main thing – but if there's only about three or four bouncers you just have to look after yourself, and still try and keep order. One particular night there was a couple of gangs in this club I was working at, the Rockhouse, and everything went haywire. They all started fighting and I got an axe in my head. It just took the top off my head like the top of an egg being cut off. Blood spurted out and I fell onto this pool table. I got the pool cue and I spun round with it and hit my attacker on the side of the head and knocked him out. Then another lad jumped on my back and I beat him up. Then the rest of the bouncers came and helped me out. That guy had cracked my skull, he chipped my bone with an axe – quite like a meat cleaver, like butchers have. They're bastards, these Hell's

Angels, they always carry weapons, so if you fight one you've got to expect to be hit by something.

'Someone phoned the police and said, "Oh, we're in trouble up at the Rockhouse," but the police didn't take it seriously. They said, "Yeah, we'll come up, we'll send three lads up." So three coppers arrived and they opened the door, looked inside and saw these bike gangs had got axes, swords, knives and everything and inside the club it was a bloodbath. So the police just said they were going for reinforcements. They ran out and they went for backup, but when they came back half an hour later it was all finished and the gang had gone. But there were about five or six ambulances outside, full of bleeding, injured people. There wasn't enough room for all the injured. That was a really flying night, know what I mean? On a scale of one to ten on the violence chart I would place that episode near the ten mark.'

Compared to that episode the approaching unlicensed fight Decca was about to have must seem easy for him, it probably wouldn't even register on the scale. I began to realise that for people who are exposed to extreme violence at that high end of the scale all the time, anything less must seem okay to them. Getting the top of your head cut off by an axe-wielding biker would certainly be ten in my book. For Decca, who survived the attack and managed to fight back, it was not the worst thing that could have happened to him. 'Near the ten mark' he'd said. To him and men like him, to be cut with a knife or hit with an axe was not unusual or outrageous. OK, it wasn't nice but it did happen, he survived and it helped his reputation. So it's not just about handing out punishment, it's also about how much you can take.

Decca says: 'Really, the deal is that in unlicensed fighting they let it go a little bit further than they would in normal professional fighting. If I was to head-butt somebody I would probably get disqualified in normal professional fighting. But the unlicensed fighting, probably not. My lifestyle, with bouncing every night and debt collecting and things like that, it kind of fits my character. That's why I'm fighting for the world title – and I think I'll come home with the belt.

'Bare-knuckle fighting is completely different. It's not boxing, it's street fighting with some rules. They do it around Tipton and Dudley and I've got one in Nottingham coming up soon with some Hell's Angel that looks as if it's on the cards. If you're the man and you can beat ten lads up and you're the street fighter of that particular part of Nottingham or whatever, that gives you quite a reputation. They think they're capable of winning a thousand pounds off me for that fight, which I'll put on the table. If he does beat me he'll take my thousand pounds and walk away but if I beat him I'll walk away with a grand. You must have the confidence to do that and there ain't many people up to doing the bare-knuckle thing. So you can't really make a living out of it. That's why you have to do the bouncing and the unlicensed fighting as well to make a good living. For 30 years that's been my lifestyle. I've taken some punches, some cuts, I come home bleeding, but it is what I like to do. Violence is like a drug to me, it's my drug.'

Looking at this great bear of a man I wondered how long he could keep going. At 44 he was still as strong as an ox but he must feel the ravages of time.

'You do get out of puff fighting, obviously. Everybody who's had a fight is out of puff within a minute and I've got to do 30 minutes. You have to have the cardiovascular fitness as well as the strength, stamina, courage and speed. So you have to do different kinds of training, like weight training, running, sparring, skipping, hitting the bag, ground work – you can't leave anything out. It all has to be done if you're to make a decent fighter.

'Well, I've always been very physical and actually I was into running the mile at school and things like that. Then I went to Burton Athletic Club and I did the cross-country running but I got too heavy, I kept putting a stone on every year. I got to like 14st and everybody else was like 10st. So I went to the Newell Boxing Club and I had a word with Jack Bodell who was the British champion then and he told me I'd be all right boxing, so I sparred with him a bit and I did

OK and I took it from there. I've never stopped – I had about 50 amateur fights and then Jack asked me if I wanted to make some money out of it, so I went professional and at the same time I started bouncing.

'I had about a hundred professional fights and I lost about fifteen. I've had five bare-knuckle fights and things like that and it's been a good experience. All the fighting has, but it's what I do – I would not know what to do if I stopped fighting and training. I would be like a fish out of water.'

Decca takes every fight seriously and his preparation has not changed much over the years.

'Before I go into the ring I focus on my opponent and what I'm going to do in the first round – obviously in the first round you go at it 'cos everybody wants to prove themselves and dominate the situation. You go forward: "Attack, attack, attack." That's what goes round my mind when I climb into the ring. It's pretty simple – you just go forward and stick your arms out and then it's basic fighting, all the rest is a load of crap really.

'The guy I'm fighting is the hard man of New York. If he's the man, I've got to do him and that's all there is to it. I don't dwell too much on how good he is. I just know how I'll fight him, how strong I am and how much stamina I've got. If you start building the other guy up you've lost straight away. I try and build myself up and concentrate on his weak points. On the night I'm going to rush at him, throw so many punches that he will not survive. If he does go five rounds he'll be very lucky. I'll just try and take him out, rip his head off in the first round. No bullshit, I'm going to have to. You can't keep a constantly running forward 19st off you for long. I'm going to punch him shitless.'

Despite being heavily pregnant, Vikki was going along with a group of friends to support Decca.

'Yes, she'll be coming on the day. The lads will come along with me on the first day for the interview and the weigh-in and she'll come down with her friends the next day for the fight. We'll have one or two buses arranged. I got a lot of friends who'll be coming down and so I should have plenty of fans there cheering me on.'

Decca is a fan of Alan's events. 'They are fantastic. The sound system and the music makes it all. When you walk into the room like that the sound system is perfect. It's like your heart's jumping out of your chest 'cos it's so deep – *bomp, bomp, bomp*. And that gets your adrenaline pumping. The kind of music they play is perfect, Big Al's got it spot-on, I must congratulate him, it really gets you psyched up.'

Decca is keen to point out that his background and the place he lives has made him what he is. 'Traditionally it's pretty hard up in the Midlands. Newell's like the hardest, roughest village in Britain really. You've got Toxteth and all those places but this is the place where the mean people are and the best fighters come from. You've got loads of really good fighters here. I'm proud to come from Swadlincote, Derby, really proud. I want to put Swadlincote on the map, like Jack Bodell (who was also born there) did when he went to Wembley and he beat Joe Bugner and got the British title. I'm going to do the same with this New York geezer. I'll beat the crap out of him and I'll have the world title and Swadlincote will be on the map again.'

I think Decca was genuinely amazed at the damage that had been done to him – and that he had survived it all.

'One professional fight I had I took a bad cut. This lad hit me with a right hook and it connected just below the eye and a cut opened up from one side of my eye right round to the other. I can still see the lad's reaction. He backed away from me going, "What the fuck's up with him?" and the referee came over and said, "Jesus Christ!" and I got stitched up. It's a rum game this fighting . . .'

In the kitchen Vikki was preparing to feed Decca. She told me: 'I'm doing Dec's raw eggs. He has twelve raw eggs every day – five with a drink of Mega Mass [a weight-gain supplement] and porridge with molasses for breakfast, and then he has one more raw egg for dinner with his steak along with another Mega Mass and then he has another three raw eggs for his tea, perhaps with a jacket potato and more Mega Mass, and then the same again before he goes to bed. It's a full-time job – he finishes one meal and starts on another. It's like that all day – worse than a kid, really. He has a lot of sweet potatoes too. They're good for energy. He has absolutely no junk food whatsoever which is quite a good thing. He only eats stuff to keep his energy up, stuff high in protein and carbohydrate.

'He's been doing extra training recently so he's a little bit more aggressive, but this is his biggest fight yet, I think. In the last fight he'd thought the decision was his but it went against him in the end and he lost. So I think he's determined. He's going to get this one this time. He'll make sure he gets it. He's just going to go forward and try to knock him out. He'll be terribly disappointed if he doesn't. I'm quietly confident that he's going to.'

It was hard to imagine how Decca courted Vikki and how Vikki fell for a man who was always fighting. 'I first met Derek when he was working at a nightclub in Derby. He had a set-to with one of my family and Derek hurt him quite badly, he broke four of his ribs. Eventually that was forgotten about and 13 years later, here we are, still together! He was fighting before he met me so it all comes with the package. But I'm happy about him fighting in the ring. It's a bit more controlled. Sometimes he comes home after a shift bouncing and he wakes up and he's covered in stitches and that puts me off. I say, "Oh my God, you could have died!" I stress but he's chilled out. He's very calm. I think it's only his calmness that keeps me sane.

'I do go and watch him fight. I've been to a few. I'm all right till I see him come into the ring. As soon as he comes in I get palpitations. I think I'm more nervous than he is, it's hard to imagine what's going through his head. But he says he has to just look after himself. He's got a job to do and that's it. The last time, I made a bit of a fool of myself. I lost the plot a bit and went absolutely crazy. Everyone was confident he was going to get the decision and he didn't get it and it was really quite upsetting. Everybody who watched the video afterwards said it was his fight.

'I think all the wives know what their husband's job is – they've all got a family to feed, haven't they? So if they don't like it they should discuss it with their husbands. They know that they're taking a gamble when their husbands go into the ring. They know what the worst possible outcome could be, so we're all in the same boat, really. I expect Derek to get a little bit hurt – you know, a few cuts and bruises, and the other wives should expect the same.

'Derek's got a reputation of being a bit of a hard case, a bit mental. But he's not a psychopath, he's just a normal person. If anyone upsets any of his family it gets his back up, but he's not a knife-wielding maniac like people might think. He just makes people give me a bit more respect, you know?

'I will definitely be going to this fight. I have about ten weeks left before my baby's born. I think that adds to the stress a little bit, you know? I've not just got myself to look after, I've got a baby as well. When I see Derek getting hit I try not to focus on that bit, I try to focus on him doing the hitting, you know what I'm saying? But it'll be the last fight I manage to get to for quite a bit so I have to make the most of it.

'He trains all the time. He gets up at the crack of dawn and runs in the morning at 5 a.m. In between training he's always topping up with food. He's trained every day since I've known him but this is mega stuff. I wouldn't say he's become selfish but he's certainly focused. This fight is going to benefit me as well as him – I want him to come home with the belt and I'm fairly sure he's going to.

'When I was about to give birth to my little girl, Tara, he left me and went to work, bouncing. He came back and she was born about ten minutes later; when I was in labour with Jake he was doing training on the bag and he said, "Wait till I've finished this round!" and so I waited till he'd finished and then he took me to hospital – just in time again! So that's dedication for you.

'One time he was due to go and see one of Lee's [Decca's son] fights and he was upstairs getting ready. I was walking down in the garden and I tripped and broke my ankle badly. All the time the cogs were turning in his head, he was thinking, how can I get to this fight? There's dedication again! He took me to the hospital and asked them,

"How long is she going to be?" And they said, "About four days in hospital." And he was thinking, oh, I'm going to miss a fight! I was lying in a hospital bed, screaming, being given morphine, everything. But he just had to get to the fight. As it turned out, though, in the end he didn't quite make it.'

TEN

IN THE END, VIKKI NEVER DID SEE DECCA FIGHT MIKE MIDDLETON. Mike never made it to Britain. Unfortunately for Alan he backed out at the last minute. The story behind Mike's decision is quite a remarkable one and it helps to highlight the relationship between the unlicensed and licensed game.

While we were filming Mike in Florida he told my director Alan Howard that he would not be fighting on Alan's bill. This was a shock, as obviously we were expecting to see Mike take on Decca at the Epping Forest Country Club, but his mind was made up. We couldn't work it out and nor could Alan when we told him. Alan had already explained to Mike that it was an unlicensed (or 'unaffiliated' in American terms) fight, but that had seemed to present no problem for Mike. But then something changed. Mike had decided to contact the Florida State Boxing Commission. They are the organisation responsible for licensing boxers in the state of Florida. They in turn contacted the British Board of Boxing Control who told them that if Mike fought on the unlicensed bill they would not give him a licence to fight in the UK again. Mike also told us that the Florida State Boxing Commission would revoke his licence for Florida specifically and this was unacceptable to him, not being able to fight in his home state.

NATURAL BORN FIGHTERS

Alan couldn't believe this. He was angry that the fight was not going to happen – the posters had all been printed with Mike's picture on them, tickets had been sold already, and what was he supposed to tell Decca Simpkin?

Resourceful as ever, Alan soon found an answer to the problem. He contacted a very good heavyweight by the name of Shane Stanton. Shane and Alan had worked together in the past in kick boxing and boxing events. Shane could always be counted on to take a fight at short notice.

Part of the reason for this was that Shane kept himself fit. He was a solid individual, not afraid of anything or anyone. After some haggling, Shane agreed to step in for Mike Middleton, thereby avoiding a major catastrophe. That's unlicensed fighting for you – most people who buy tickets haven't heard of many of the men on the bill, so occasionally when one of the advertised fighters doesn't turn up, they're not worried. They know that fighters get ill, scared or arrested. But they also know that they'll have a good, entertaining night no matter what. But that was not the end of the Mike Middleton story.

Some months after Alan's event had taken place, Audley Harrison, Britain's next big heavyweight hope, was due to take his first professional fight. It was a crucial one for him. The hopes of the nation were pinned on him and he had to give a good performance. The press were speculating who the opponent might be. Then about a week before the fight it was announced that Audley Harrison would be fighting a boxer from Florida – none other than Mike Middleton. We'll never really know exactly what happened but it is likely it went like this. Mike was all set to fight on Alan's unlicensed bill but he got a call from Audley's people and was offered the fight with him. Mike will have told them that he had already committed to another fight, Alan's unlicensed one, and they told him that if he fought on an unlicensed bill he wouldn't be able to take a licensed fight again in the UK. So Mike will have decided that it would be better for his career if he fought Audley Harrison rather than Decca Simpkin.

Despite a distraction at the time, involving his wife handing him divorce papers, Mike Middleton kept his licence and was selected to take on Britain's Olympic gold medallist Audley Harrison at Wembley Arena on 19 May 2001. The fight did not last long as Mike was way out of his depth and got knocked down more than once. He fought on bravely but could not stop the younger, stronger, heavier man. In short, it was a mismatch. As for Mike, well, perhaps he would have been better off fighting Decca for a title. After all, a fighter in his late 30s is not likely to get another title shot.

So now, for Decca and Shane Stanton the fight was on. Decca had come down to Essex with a large following. Vikki, his wife, was heavily pregnant. She looked like she was about to pop! She was frightened that too much excitement might bring on the pregnancy, so the paramedics were warned. Decca had brought his sons with him too, both of them professional fighters and both huge lads. After all, Decca himself was not small. He was a giant of a man and even at 44 years of age he looked formidable. He towered over most of the other fighters in the gym above the nightclub at the Epping Forest Country Club.

Decca's fight with Shane Stanton would be the main event of the evening and Decca would have to wait for all the other fights to take place before he came on. But he kept himself busy, largely by eating. He had a strict pre-fight diet, which he seemed to be sticking to rigidly. This consisted of Mars bars and coffee with lots of sugar. As the time drew closer for Decca to fight he became increasingly nervous. His toilet trips increased and his shouting could be heard over the music downstairs.

Of course only recently being told that you are not fighting the man you thought you were going to fight is a bit unsettling. Alan seemed to think he was handling it well.

'He was all right about it, Decca, he didn't really care either way, but Vikki was concerned that home-boy Shane would get the decision. But I don't work like that – I work with all these different promoters and fighters and I have to be fair. But Vikki said she wanted me in Decca's corner. Now I know straight away that when someone wants me in their corner, they're really saying that they're going to win. But it doesn't matter which corner I'm in – it doesn't affect the outcome either way.'

Decca was afraid that he might get another bad decision. Vikki was philosophical about the news that he was going to have to fight another opponent. 'Decca always says never make plans,' she told me. 'Anyway, you know who you're fighting when they're there and in your face. He's just got to do what he's got to do, I suppose.'

Despite the short notice Shane was cool, calm and collected. He prepared himself for this fight as he did for any other one. He warmed up, relaxed, shadow boxed, worked on the pads and kept loose. He said: 'I'll go with whatever the fighter wants to do. If he wants to box, we'll box; if he wants a brawl, we'll brawl. Whatever way, I'm very adaptable and we'll go from there.'

Although they had come to terms with the change in opponent, backstage, Decca and his family were dealing with other general pre-fight stress. As well as the belt there was a one thousand pound prize at stake and Decca could not help but think about it and what he had to do to get it.

Decca was getting psyched-up. 'Fucking one thousand pounds. *Bastard!*' he said. A cash prize and a title belt on the line, then, for Derek Simpkin, the giant doorman from Derby and his wife Vikki. 'I will be very glad to see the end of this, yeah,' he says. 'I'll be glad to take that belt home, I've made a space for it already. No pressure though, eh?' For Decca the moment of truth was coming. 'Ten fucking rounds. I'm a lunatic! I'm a fucking lunatic!'

After months of preparation, the moment the crowd have been waiting for arrives. Derek Simpkin steps up to claim Alan Mortlock's WPA super heavyweight championship of the world. It's time for Vikki to start worrying.

Shane was the first to be called into the ring. He waited calmly for Decca to walk in. Decca came into the bubbling cauldron of the

Atlantis bar to roars from his fans from Derby, who by this time were a little worse for wear from drink. His hands were placed on one of his sons' shoulders in front of him and he was already sweating.

Referee Gary Bedford called them to the centre of the ring.

'All right gentlemen, I expect a nice clean one tonight. When I say break I want you to break and step out cleanly. I'm not going to stand for anything in here, all right lads? Shake hands and have a good one.'

The bell sounded for round one and it was a cautious start by both men. This was to be expected – they were, after all, scheduled to fight ten rounds.

After the first round Derek looked a little the worse for wear. Shane, on the other hand, looked as fresh as a daisy. If Decca was going take this fight, clearly he'd have to land some pretty serious punches and go for a knockout. But by this stage nobody had landed a clean punch.

The second round did not get much better. It may have been an unlicensed fight but Decca was not getting away with much. Gary Bedford pulled him up time and time again for low punches and for holding onto the ropes.

By the third round, though, the pattern of the fight was set. The bell went and Decca came straight at Shane. Shane was able to fire off two shots, but he was then smothered by Derek's massive arms. Most of Derek's work was done inside, with his head rubbing in Shane's face, or hitting him low. The younger man could not get free to hit cleanly. This went on round after round. True to his word, Decca kept coming forward. He pushed, round after round. He tied Shane up, sapping his energy. This might seem to be a good tactic – after all Shane was a younger man. You could see that he was getting exhausted by having this bear of a fighter leaning all over him. Perhaps Decca's master plan was to come on strong at the end – but sadly it was not to be. By the end, I realised what Decca meant by stamina. He looked as though he was about to fall over, but he always managed to stay on his feet. Shane tried everything to break free but he was always frustrated. The pace of the fight never lifted above the pedestrian and the few good few punches that were thrown were Shane's.

After 27 minutes of pushing, shoving – and not much boxing – we had reached the last but one round. That belt had to go to someone. For Vikki it was almost all too much to bear. She was sure that Decca was going to win. 'Oooh, one more to go!' she said.

'Seconds out – tenth and final round,' announced the referee.

Shane came out from his corner all smiles. In that smile he was saying to Decca, 'Well done, you've survived the rounds, you stopped me from knocking you out – let's just get through the next one.' You could see Decca had relaxed. His shoulders had dropped, so too had his hands and his chin had lifted. This was exactly what Shane was waiting for.

They touched gloves and once the referee had said 'box' Shane aimed a massive, arcing right hand at Decca's head. Shane was leaning forward, his feet planted firmly on the canvas. It was a punch that had floored many opponents in the past. It was well practised and when the timing was right it could be devastating. All of his weight was behind the punch and to the audience it seemed to be in the air for a lifetime. Any contact with Decca's head would have meant the end of him. No one could have survived it.

But it missed.

Decca had shuffled forwards. He'd tucked his chin in and as he swayed to the right, at the last minute Decca slightly adjusted his position and just managed to slip the shot. It glanced off his head and fell away towards his shoulder. Decca was stunned by the ferocity of the punch though, and blinked with surprise. But he recovered again and pushed in close to Shane. Shane was now on the back foot, being pushed backwards and the normal rhythm of the fight resumed. Decca held on for the rest of the round and smothered Shane's attempts to strike cleanly.

Decca had survived the ten three-minute rounds – and Vikki was feeling confident. Steve Holdsworth, the master of ceremonies, climbed into the ring, microphone in hand, and summed the fight up perfectly.

'I'm sure you'll agree that that was an exceptionally difficult fight to watch. Let's have a look at the score . . . 97 points to 96 . . . your winner, and new super heavyweight champion of the world . . . Shane Stanton!'

It was all over for Decca's title dream. The local lad had got the decision, leaving Decca, his fans and Vikki not very happy.

A Decca supporter summed up his feelings: 'What happened to the true spirit of fighting, coming forward with the aggression, where was it? Where was it tonight?'

Vikki was heartbroken. 'Another bad decision,' she said. 'I don't think we'll be coming back, it was a bit unfair.'

The night at the Epping Forest Country Club was over. Even before Shane had lifted his belt in front of the crowds, the Atlantis bar was emptying. It had been a night to remember, full of drama. We had seen courage and bravery, disappointment and pain. There was the joy of winning and the heartache of losing; scores settled and bad blood created. Amongst the crowd of family and friends, there were a few who wanted to fight on the next bill themselves. And that was what it was all about – anyone could fight if they wanted to enough, if they wanted to train and get fit. This was open to anyone who had the courage to step into the ring and fight.

For Alan, the night had been a success on all levels. 'I'm over the moon,' he said, 'it's launched our organisation properly.' And as we spoke Alan Mortlock was organising another monster boxing event at a location somewhere in Essex . . . book now to avoid disappointment!

So after all that Decca never did get his belt. He went back to Derby and is now the proud father of a baby boy named Jack – after Jack Dempsey, the former heavyweight champion of the world.

ELEVEN

OF COURSE ALAN'S EVENTS ARE NOT THE ONLY TYPES OF FIGHTING going on. We found many more that were much more extreme than anything we had ever seen before. One of these types was something that went by the name of 'no holds barred'. This is a mixed style of fighting that allowed fighters to kick, punch, wrestle and choke.

Leigh Ramedios is 24 years old. He is an electronic engineering student at the University of Kent in Canterbury, and he is a natural born fighter. He told me: 'I do get a craving for it, you know? I get an itch. To me there's just something electric about it. Fighting is fighting, it's not a sport. It's not a matter of, "You can't do this, you can't do that, here's the rules." A fight's a fight. It's simple. You see who's the better fighter.'

Leigh is a kid who can smell a scrap. That's why he was in Vancouver in 1997, as one of the few Brits daring to take on the North Americans at a new no-rules, no holds barred fighting phenomenon. In America a sport they call 'ultimate fighting' there became popular. The advertisements warned that 'there are no rules, no judges, no scores and no time limits'. This new fighting form first found infamy in America in 1993. The idea was to pit all combat styles against each other. Anything went. The Americans even came up with a new octagonal ring to hold these fights in. The outcome, of course – total carnage. In the last eight years two men have died at events abroad.

Ultimate fighting was banned in 49 American states but once created the idea soon spread to countries like Japan, Russia and Canada, where our boy Leigh became an eager student.

Leigh told me: 'I did one time put a guy in an arm-bar and he held on for ages. He didn't tap, and he had been a bit aggressive with me so I didn't feel any guilt about it, and I cranked it a little bit harder. I can't think of any other explanation about what happened next other than his arm broke.'

For readers who don't know what an arm-bar is, it's worth explaining. Straighten your arm out in front of you. Now turn your palm to the ceiling. Now imagine that someone has placed your upper arm in a vice and the vice is closed tightly around it, gripping your bicep just above your elbow. Your hand is hanging free and you can bend it at the elbow and raise your hand upwards. Now imagine that vice is a man, roughly your own weight, wrapping both his legs around your upper arm, gripping it between his thighs. He is now holding onto your wrist with both his hands too. Now he leans back, still holding onto your wrist. All his weight is now putting unbelievable pressure on your elbow joint. If you can imagine that, you can begin to imagine what it might feel like to be on the receiving end of an arm-bar. Once it is applied it is almost impossible to get out of and the pain is said to be unbearable. In a short time it feels as though your arm could break at the elbow at any time.

After Canada, Leigh returned to England where, in the last four years, no holds barred has caught on. It's completely legal but it is outside the authority of the traditional martial arts world. In the UK promoters decide their own rules; you could say the style is a law unto itself – which suited Leigh down to the ground.

Leigh said: 'As soon as I heard about the no holds barred stuff I thought to myself, that's exactly what fighting needs – just mixing everything up, you know? No tradition, you get in there and you see what combat really is. When I compete I'm just whipping these guys because they haven't been exposed to the sort of training that I have.'

For no holds barred you need to get smart on two counts – grappling and punching. Leigh was a man who liked to fight from the floor, forcing his opponents to submit – 'tapping out' as it's known. But in no holds barred you can also punch.

Leigh says: 'I don't think that you get a chance to strike so much in no holds barred, you know? When you're trying to kick a guy and he's trying to wrestle you it's very awkward. You're off balance. You can't just land the blows that cause damage when a guy is trying to grapple with you.'

For Leigh the ring has always been his second classroom. He's trained in judo, ju-jitsu, karate, kick boxing and tae kwon do. For fighters like him the training has to be as close to the real deal as it can get. The only way to learn is the hard way.

'Pain? It is all in the mind' he says. 'You have to be able to take a beating, and then another and another, and not quit. I train for it so I'm used to it, you know? These guys in the ring they're only going to do it to me for ten, fifteen minutes. I'm getting it all the time when I'm training so it's not a big deal.'

Leigh's been in training since he was a toddler. His mum realised what he was like from an early age. She told me: 'He's had a bit of aggression in him ever since he was born and luckily . . . well, he's had a few black eyes and things haven't you? But nothing really . . . serious.'

Leigh adds: 'My dad always had me punching and kicking, you know, learning basic fighting skills as I soon as I was learning to walk.'

Leigh's dad now lives in Canada and was Leigh's corner-man during his Vancouver fights. Leigh says: 'He did a lot of fighting when he was younger and he taught me a fight was a fight, you know, just beating someone up. He taught me that you can win, no matter how big you are or how strong you are – although the techniques he showed me, like stamping on people's hands on the floor, that's a bit sneaky.'

There was a British, no holds barred tournament scheduled for the following weekend by the name of Vale Tudo. Leigh explains: 'Vale Tudo is a Portuguese term from Brazil that literally means "everything is valid". You can do whatever you like. You can head-butt, you can elbow, you can knee. All submissions are legal. The only thing is that there's no biting and no eye gouging – that's usually about it. You have to think to yourself when you're in there that – yeah – you *are* indestructible. You have to believe that you can't be hurt. It's my training that makes me believe that I won't get beat because the guy's not gonna be able to pull his moves off on me. He won't be able to arm-bar me and break my arm, or choke me till I'm unconscious, because I'm a better fighter. I don't go out there and think I'm gonna win carelessly. I know these guys can do damage if I let them, but I'm not gonna let them. I know what I've got to do, I've got to take care of business.'

The Vale Tudo tournament that Leigh was taking part in was being held in Bedfont in London. When he got there, Leigh weighed in at 12st 6lb but he was told that the opponent he was supposed to have been fighting hadn't turned up, and there was no one else in his weight category for him to take on.

Leigh said: 'I ended up being lighter than I expected and everyone else has weighed in heavy so it's not looking good as far as an opponent goes. Still, I'd like to do it today, you know? I'd like to get in there and show them what we've got.'

Just in case he found a match, Leigh decided to get au fait with the rules of the tournament. Andy Jardine, the event organiser and promoter of mixed martial arts events, which were sanctioned by the British Judo Association, took questions from various fighters.

'Can you elbow and knee the body?'

'I'll say it one more time – there will be no elbows at all, OK? *At all!*' Andy said.

'Hands on the face?'

'Yeah, you can do that.'

Leigh was not impressed – this tournament was meant to be Vale Tudo so anything was supposed to be valid. But, in practice, promoter Andy Jardine was imposing strict rules. Leigh demonstrated a move that looked like he would snap another guy's neck.

Andy Jardine did not approve. 'You've got the guy like that, then flip him over into the sash and hold? To start with it's all right but when you start bending him back, you begin straining the spine – so, no, that's not allowed. When you see that guy in a wheelchair two years later with his daughters around him you'll be thinking – shit. And then it'll start to hit you what you've done.'

But for Leigh any rules at all were a let down. He said, 'I train for no holds barred, right? I wouldn't use "the guillotine" like that anyway so it's no problem for me – I'm just saying that too many rules detracts from the no holds barred side of it.'

But Andy, a veteran fighter himself, knew better. 'The thing is that no holds barred isn't really no holds barred anymore, it's changed. It's now mixed martial arts.'

Leigh wasn't too happy with Andy's argument – but then there was one bit of good news – it turned out he'd got an opponent, although he was a bit on the small side.

'He seems like a nice kid,' said Leigh, 'but I'm gonna fuckin' ruin him! He's just under 11st. I don't see how a guy that small could possibly hope to beat me. It's gonna be silly. I shouldn't really be matched against him.'

As the tournament got underway, despite the rules, the crowd were about to see some truly brutal action. But according to promoter Andy Jardine people are not getting the whole story. He explained to me his views on the tournament: 'I was just sick of going to bad promotions and couldn't believe how badly they were run. So I thought I'll do it properly and I'd make sure the fighters were looked after properly, that they wouldn't just be left in the changing-room on a mat with nothing to drink. And that's just one example – I mean some shows I've been to have had no doctor there. There were shows where people just got robbed of their titles in that ring. Most of the time they just shouldn't have been but they were just robbed in the end. That's basically what started me doing it. I thought, right, I'm going to do my own one, I'm going to do it properly and make sure everyone is looked after.

'Of all the tournaments I've been to to fight, I've actually been treated the best in America – and Russia, believe it or not. I've never been treated too well over here. So I've made it a point that I'll never fight here myself again. I'll always take a fight abroad, but not in England.'

Andy had had his fare share of injury. 'Oh, I had my teeth knocked out with an elbow, which is something that shouldn't have happened, as elbows shouldn't be allowed. I've knocked people out, unconscious, and should have won the fight but they've let the guy have a long count and they've carried on. And it's disheartening, that kind of thing, because I've put a lot of training into this, I've put a lot of work into it. I've worked hard to make my skills good and there are too many times I've felt like I should have won it and I've been robbed. That's why I don't want that to happen to anyone else, that's why I started doing my own promotions and I'm trying to make it much fairer for everyone else.'

Andy explains: 'I don't allow any spinal locks at all. I don't allow any suplexes (which involves people landing on the back of the head). It's got to be a clean throw when they land on their back, just like in judo. Safety is my major priority. I want to make sure about that for my benefit, and for the fighter's benefit – I want to see him again and I want to make sure I can promote again. That's important. If anything goes wrong it means the thing can't happen again. It means it won't happen again for me and it won't happen again for anyone else, so I must make sure nothing really bad ever happens. I'm very strict about the rules. They're allowed to kick to the legs and the head. You don't see that very often though, because there's a lot of grappling and they intertwine so quickly that there's not much scope for a head kick. If they're wearing wrestling boots, they're not allowed to kick with their wrestling boots because the laces on them can tear the skin.

'The fighters wear small, padded gloves. But they're not padded so that people don't get cut like some people may imagine. The padding is minimal because you need to get your hand in there for the strangleholds and for the arm-locks and stuff. If you're wearing big gloves you can't do any of that and also there's more punching with a big glove – if you can't get the submission you want you end up punching and I want to get away from that. I want them to use a small padded glove so people get proper submissions.

'You're allowed punches to the head when standing, just like in boxing. But you're also allowed to punch to the head when you're on the ground. When people see this they often see one guy sitting on top of another in a dominant position – which is called the "mount"– and they see that guy punching the guy underneath him and they feel sorry for the guy underneath because they think he's losing. But it doesn't always work like that. The guy underneath can often come back and win, you know? It's actually the guy that's punching who is actually vulnerable at that stage. He can be turned at any time and the whole fight will just change around. Often he's aware of that, so he won't be punching that hard. He'll be more likely looking for a submission from the mount. When you're in the mount position, punching, you can never punch that hard anyway because your arm only gives you 20 per cent of your punching power. To generate the rest you have to be on your feet. And that's why I don't allow someone on their feet punching someone on the ground. They always have to be on the same level. Both the attacker's knees have to be touching the floor if he is punching. He can't be up on one knee or standing up because then he can generate more power because he's got gravity on his side and his body weight is moving down. So I don't allow that either.

'Me and another promoter, we use the same rules. A lot of kick boxing promoters will ring us up and ask us about our rules, so ideally we all use the same ones. But basically we're more organised than the kick boxers.

'There will be an authority in the future but it won't be made up of promoters. They'll be impartial to promotions to make it fair. If you're a promoter I don't think it's fair for you to monopolise an industry. An authority will be set up that everyone's going to be part of. Things won't go the same way as kick boxing. It's going to be organised. It's going to be done properly.

'We're all starting to use the same medical forms which are going to be endorsed by a medical company. I've got fight clearance forms, disclaimer forms, that kind of thing. We'll probably use the same paramedics for every show as well, so that they're familiar with the fighters and with what goes on.

'We've brought a lot of other people to other sports like judo and kick boxing. People go to several classes to learn the different techniques fairly. They go to a Vale Tudo class or a submission wrestling class but they'll also go to a judo class as well. You'll find that some people will probably enjoy the judo more than the Vale Tudo and they'll stick with that. That's good for the country because we need a few more judo fighters out there, you know? And people want to do kick boxing too, it gets them fit. I've got a few girls that train down my club. They love kick boxing. All that kicking keeps their legs slim and their bum trim. They're actually learning something at the same time, too. It's not just like an aerobics class where they just stop doing it after a month and that's it. If they stop doing this after a month, then perhaps they'll not be as fit, but they've learnt something by at least starting it. They've learnt how to defend themselves a little bit which is always important. People always think, it's never going to happen to me – but those are famous last words. You never know. Everyone should be able to protect themselves. I mean, for Christ's sake, the country protects itself with weapons and battleships and all sorts of stuff like that, so if the country's doing it, surely the individuals in that country should do the same. It doesn't mean you're a bad person because you do martial arts to protect yourself, just as it doesn't mean you're a bad country because you've got nuclear weapons to protect yourself, you know? You're just protecting yourself that's all, it's your right.

'We're bringing everyone together, from all different martial arts backgrounds. You'll get a guy in a Vale Tudo fight who's from a judo background, one from a kick boxing background and someone else from yet another background. If I had to say what my background was it would be judo first, then it'd be kick boxing. Our fights just bring everyone together.

'I think people who are wondering about our fights sometimes get a bit confused when they see these two guys hugging each other on the floor. They wonder why one's just belting the other and they immediately disapprove. But I think that if they just became educated to the rules, they would enjoy it – because there's so many ways that people can win. And it really is exciting to watch. If we get coverage on TV a little bit, people could see it. They could always choose whether they want to turn over or not, just like they can choose to turn over if they see a plane crash with loads of dead burning bodies, or a load of guys that have been squashed at a football match or something. They can just turn over. I think we should get it on the television. People should be able to watch it if they want to watch it. It's a free country. We should be able to put it on TV. If the Sports Council got behind it, it'd be even better because then it'd definitely be regulated properly, you know? That would be really good.

'I'd say our stuff is more WWF. I'd say it's more about the characters – like Leigh Ramedios and Ian Freeman. There's loads of great characters for people to follow. They're great, great guys. Lots of the appeal of WWF lies in the appeal of the characters.

'I think because of our background in martial arts, there's a lot of etiquette and honour involved. I think you get that with boxing as well, sometimes in the professional ranks but I'm not too sure. I wouldn't like to say, to be honest, because I've only ever been to a boxing club once. I prefer the martial arts. But that's just my opinion, you know? Everyone's entitled to their own and that's just mine.'

I asked Andy what sort of person he thinks you have to be to fight in a sport that has so few rules. 'I would say that the boxers do well, they seem to be the most intelligent in general. Those guys tend to think more than the brawlers. You could say that Mike Tyson's a

NATURAL BORN FIGHTERS

brawler but you'd be wrong because really he's a thinker. He's a very intelligent man and a lot of other guys I could mention, the famous boxers, are all very intelligent and they're the ones that seem to do best. Within Vale Tudo, you need to be intelligent to learn the moves because there's thousands of them. They're endless. There's a move off this move off that move – and they all interconnect. You need to be able to move from one to another. You need to be up for punches and kicks together. You need to be ready for throws, take downs and ground fighting. You need to be able to get up from the ground whenever you can. There's a lot involved so it does take a bit of thought. So I would say in general that it takes an intelligent man to learn the grappling skills.'

I ask Andy how it's connected to 'bare knuckle'. He replies: 'Well, when it first started as "the ultimate fighting championships", it was banned in a lot of states because they weren't using any gloves; it was pretty much "anything goes". People complained, so they had to tighten up the regulations. They're now actually working with the boxing people out there in America. They're very, very strict. I just came back from an ultimate fighting championship about two or three weeks ago where one of my friends, Ian Freeman, was fighting and it was so well run. I was really impressed.

'They have to give a blood test now before they fight. If their blood tests for anything, you know, like AIDS or something like that, they can't compete ever again. They have to give a urine sample too, so they can't be on any drugs or anything.

'They're very, very strict and their rules have changed a lot as well. UFC, the Ultimate Fighting Championship, is an American mixed martial arts championship which has been going for many years. Some of the best mixed martial arts fighters in the world are attracted to the UFC and it is the ultimate goal of British fighters to be invited along to fight there. The only Brit to have done this to date is Ian Freeman.

'In the early days, these fights were very brutal and anything went. They took place in a cage. It was banned from many states. But, gradually, the rules were changed and now it is one of the best mixed martial arts events in the world. It all started in Brazil. A lot of people were into martial arts there. A lot of people doing different martial arts; a lot of egos were clashing, so they thought, right – let's put on a show, let's get all the different martial arts together and let's get boxing and karate in there too. They thought, we'll do kung fu and we'll test out our ju-jitsu too. So they put all this in the ring and back then, they didn't even really punch. They were just using their grappling skills. But as things progressed, you got more fighters arriving from a boxing background who were very good strikers, and so the grapplers had to learn how to box because they were fighting a guy who could both grapple and punch. Then eventually kick boxers from a good kick boxing background came along who had learnt how to grapple too. That's one dangerous man! So the fighters have had to constantly adapt. It's changed a lot since the beginning, though. The standard's really gone up since then.

'Many sports fans play that "who was the best" game – like who would have won out of Ali versus Tyson; who was the better footballer, George Best or David Beckham. When Vale Tudo started out, people were asking which style of fighting was the best – boxing, kick boxing, kung fu and all the rest. Today the sport has evolved into a combination of all the styles in one fighter. Mixed martial arts is the ultimate challenge for fighters and a compelling spectator sport as well. It's just something that appeals to people. It's something new and exciting. It's like – *wow*. It combines all the martial arts in one arena. Thousands of people go to watch kick boxing, and other people go to watch Thai boxing or judo or wrestling. But in a mixed martial arts show you get it all in one. You can see it all together in one place. At the same event, you're going to see some great punchers, you're going to see some great kickers, you'll see it all. You're certainly going to get your money's worth.'

But there are those who see the sport for the first time and they think it just looks like a particularly nasty street fight. Andy says: 'It might look brutal to them if they see someone sitting on top of another guy, punching him in the head. But as I said, the arm only constitutes 20 per cent of your punching power. That's why you really only see a knockout if the guy punching is standing up, because on the ground, you've only got your arm's power, you haven't got the full power in your hips and the rest of your body movement. No one's ever been knocked out with one punch from the mount. If a guy's on the ground, he's also got the option of holding onto you. Two fighters on the ground won't be split apart by the referee like they are in some other sports and told to start again. The thing is that's human nature – when you get hit, you grab on. We've seen enough fights on TV where when someone's getting hit a lot they grab on, only to have the ref stepping in and pushing them apart so that they can clash again. This will not happen in mixed martial arts. The guy's who's getting hit can grab the other guy's arm. He can throw him to the ground instead. As I said, those punches on the ground are very, very weak compared to the punches dealt out if you're standing. You can generate a lot of power standing. And once you go to the ground it just becomes wrestling. And from then, you're looking for the submission – and everyone wants to win by submission.'

Of course Andy's right up to a point – but sometimes the man on the ground is just too tired to fight back. Then his life is in the hands of the referee. In some fights the end comes quickly, but three years ago in Kiev a man died after receiving just that punishment. But then they do have different rules in Kiev and will let things go a little further. Andy Jardine applied his own rules to his events and we were about to see what difference they had made to the fights. Leigh was the next up on the bill. He looked much bigger than his opponent but the two were just within Andy Jardine's stipulated three-kilo weight difference.

Leigh was dressed in judo kit covered with badges, a purple belt tied around his waist. He warmed up throwing punches with a constant flowing rhythm that would be punctuated by a roundhouse kick followed up with yet more punches. His movement was smooth and flowing, not jerky. It was powerful, with grace and efficient use of energy.

The ring was an ordinary boxing standard size with ropes and corner posts. Leigh stripped down to his trunks and stepped into the ring. His opponent was waiting for him there. They both wore the fingerless gloves with a small amount of padding on them. Leigh wore lightweight boots, his opponent was barefoot. The referee called out to both of them.

'Are you ready?'

Both fighters nodded.

'Let's fight.'

Leigh immediately raised his hands, open-palmed and started bouncing around on his toes. His opponent rushed at him and swung a wild punch. Leigh saw it coming, ducked, grabbed the other man around the waist, lifted him off the canvas and slammed him down onto his back. Leigh then landed on top of him. His opponent held onto the back of Leigh's head, pulling it into his own chest and gripped his upper body with his thighs. He managed to hit Leigh twice in the side of the head. Leigh grabbed his opponent's arms and held them down. At the same time he worked to get his opponent's legs off his body but they were too high up and he could not budge them. Leigh used all his strength to lift his head up and release the other man's grip. He managed to wrestle free and somehow he got into a mount. Sitting astride his opponent who was lying on the canvas, he began to smash the other man's head with his free hands, with great swinging punches. His opponent raised his own arms to protect his face and at that point Leigh saw his chance. He grabbed one of those arms and went for an arm-bar – one of Leigh's favourite moves. Remember, he had already broken someone's arm with this move when he was fighting in Canada. Leigh's opponent held on bravely for a good two minutes but the pain got too much and he tapped out. Leigh had won.

For his size Leigh was powerfully built, but he had the flexibility

NATURAL BORN FIGHTERS

that the sport demands. He told me he was running out of good opposition of similar weight in the UK.

He told me: 'They do treat you pretty well. I fought in Milton Keynes and it was really a good, really well organised event and I really liked it, but on the whole over here you can't earn the money and you can't get the prestige. I do occasionally still fight in the UK but not so much. When I was in Milton Keynes I gave away quite a bit of weight, about a stone and a half. That was where I won the belt. I'm more or less accepted as the best lightweight in the UK abroad and there's no real point in me fighting here until I get beaten over there, I'm just going through the motions. In the UK I earn more than most and that's still not a great deal. I earn a fair few hundred quid per fight, but a lot of guys don't earn that, a lot of guys are fighting for fifty quid a night or less, you know? And that's bad. A lot of it's done on ticket sales, the more tickets you sell the more you earn, you get a percentage of the sales. In the UK a decent purse often depends on how many friends you've got, really. That's never going to go big time. I mean if they've got lots of friends I guess they can earn a fair whack but not a real wage.

'As it is right now, I could earn enough money to live without having to do other work, so I could fight professionally but I can't be doing that when I'm 40 you know? And I wouldn't be mega rich. I'm a lightweight and lightweights will never earn as much as heavyweights will, it's just not going to happen.

'I'd fight in the Ultimate Fighting Championship [the UFC], they do pay so much better and you get instant fame within that circle. But I've got exams and stuff coming up – I'm going into engineering as a career. It's going to be difficult to juggle both and I have to say, the fighting will have to take second place. I mean work's always going to keep me going. I'll always fight if I get the option but it's going to have to come behind my engineering. The UFC, though – that's just the dream.

'I've got this fight coming up in Prague. I'm going there on my own, with no corner-man. I'll pay my own way to get over there but really I'm taking a bit of a risk going. We've got good contacts with the guys though, so we should be OK. But I don't really have any idea about what to expect. I've never really spent a lot of time in Europe; I've been to France, and that's about it. But I guess you just turn up and play it by ear – just beat someone up.

'My family don't really take much of an interest in my fights. They might pretend to because I get a bit of local fame in the paper and I've been on the box but to be honest, I'll get home, and it'll just be, you know – "Hi Mum I just got back," and she'll ask where I've been, and I'll say, "I've been abroad, fighting. Here's my trophy," or whatever. And she'll go, "Oh, that's nice, Son."

'The fight in Prague, as far as I'm aware, is pretty much like the original Vale Tudo. There are no real rules, just some bare bones – no biting, no eye gouging, and they've got one that says you can't use an open hand to the ear; it's fine to punch or kick to the ear but no open hands. That's it, I mean you can hit in the groin, you can head-butt, you can do everything, you know? Otherwise I've got no idea what to expect, really. I'll be fighting a guy from the Czech Vale Tudo team. He's an undefeated Thai boxer, so I'm told, so I really don't know how it's going to go. My kick boxing's not bad, I train a lot with a guy called Floyd Brown and I've been training down in Dover with some good guys as well. So we'll see how it goes, my stand-up defence is OK at least, and I don't think anyone will take me for a mug on the ground and they won't out-wrestle me. But you never know. I'll be wearing wrestling boots when I fight, I think – if I'm fighting a Thai boxer, I don't want to stand up with him too much, you know? I want to knock him down pretty quick, so I'm going to wear boots – which will stop me kicking but that doesn't really bother me because if he's a good kick boxer I don't want to waste energy kicking him anyway.

'I think this kind of fighting is no more dangerous. I think that in bare knuckle, there's no more danger of you being really hurt. There's more danger of being cut so that will probably make you quit sooner, which is a good thing. You can't take as much punishment pain-wise. I think also there are times in regular fighting when, as you're taking a beating, you just have to stand there, whereas with bare knuckle, if

I'm getting hit at least I can grab the guy and try and tie him up, you know, to save myself that beating. As long as the two fighters are skilled, I don't think it's dangerous at all. They know how to defend themselves and they'll tap out when they're in trouble.

'I have seen some shows where you get mismatches. Some guy will go in there off the street with no skills, and they might either go in there and smash some martial artist who thinks he knows it all and in fact doesn't know anything – or they end up getting hammered. I've never seen anyone brutally K.O.'d though. I've never seen anyone get their neck broken or any other stupid stories like that that you sometimes hear. I've just seen guys get a whipping but then the ref stops it and that's the end of that.

'When I was a teenager I used to scrap quite a bit. I was brought up on a council estate and I'd fight like everyone else did. I probably took to it a bit more than other people though. I flew off the handle a little bit. To be completely honest, I've had a couple of scraps since I've been fighting pro. Not that I go out and intentionally pick on guys in bars, but I've had guys try and cross me – they'd barge me or something like that but they don't know what I do for a living. So I say "Knock it off, right? I don't want to kick your arse." And that usually resolved it. But there have been a couple of times, perhaps in the last four years – I've maybe had about two or three scraps on the street. When I was younger I'd go looking for it almost – whereas now I don't need that casual scrapping; I don't *need* to go out and bash people on the street. Anyway, if people know who I am and that I fight professionally I don't get any of that stuff. They're cool with me and I'm cool with most people. Occasionally guys won't take no for an answer, but if I've retaliated it's only ever been in self-defence – but I've beaten up a couple of guys, both much bigger than me. I've popped one guy's arm. They came and had a go and I said, "Look, I'll fight you and I'll do you," and they won't have it, so pop goes the elbow – or, nighty-night, out they go.

'To be successful in the fight game I think you have to really be prepared to put up a fight. You've got to know that the risks are out there and you've just got to ignore them and go out there and kick arse. Physical attributes help of course, but they're not the be all and end all. You've got to be sharp too and I think I'm successful because I know what I'm doing; I train to get strong and for speed and stamina. But originally, everything comes from your mindset.

'I've only had one loss and that was when I was starting out as a novice. I fought a guy, who had just won the UFC actually, and I gave him a much better fight than he got in the Championships. Right now I could beat that guy though. I had one draw when I was a novice but apart from those, I've won all my fights. I've had something like 19 or 20 fights.

'I've always just liked to fight, you know? Particularly with no rules, because if you put rules in there it becomes a sport and that's not interesting to me. But I've always been fascinated to see who would win a fight between a kick boxer and a boxer or a wrestler – well, now we can find out. My old man fought too. He had a few competitions when he was younger and he did well, but he was never at the level that I'm at now.

'As a sport Vale Tudo originated so that styles could compete against styles. Originally I think it involved the Brazilian form of judo versus the Japanese form of judo and then everyone else got in on the act. As a sport it's different to just about everything else. There's practically no rules, you know, but it's different to street fighting in as much as you can quit when you want and there's only two guys fighting and there's no weapons involved. I think it's probably the best sport that would prepare you for a street fight, though, in that you'll feel comfortable wherever you are – except when it comes to being face to face with the other end of a knife, which nothing's really going to prepare you for.

'I've been fighting for about four years now professionally and my mindset has changed over the years. When I first went out there I would be full of butterflies and I just wanted to go and smash the guy up; I just wanted to go out and beat him. Now I don't hate the guy, you know? The crowd can cheer or boo, I don't care, I'm not concerned with them. I'm going out there like I would facing a tennis match or a game of football – I'm just going out there to win. I don't feel any hatred. I still get a bit of nerves from the competition, but that's about it.

'I do need to focus properly. It's the same with anything at a high level, or at this level of international competition. You have to focus yourself. You can't just be having a cup of tea and find yourself thinking, "Oh, I'm off, let's pop out for a fight," you know? You've got to psyche yourself up, you've got to train mentally as well as physically. Everyone who fights Vale Tudo has to be clued up, or they wouldn't be fighting anyway – certainly not at the level that I'm at because it takes intelligence to learn your moves and everything. Good boxers might perhaps sometimes sound a bit punch drunk, but they're clued up – all the fighters at top level are smart guys. When I started off some guys would come in to fight and they'd seem scary; everyone you fought would look hard – I mean they wouldn't necessarily actually be hard but they'd look that way 'cos these were guys who were going to beat you up. Some of them would just come out scrapping, slugging away – but you'd just have to take them apart with technique, technique, technique.

'The difference between what I do and boxing is vast. We fight in a ring; sometimes in a cage. I've fought on mats, I've fought on raised platforms, I've fought on the docks and in warehouses. But the rules are totally different too. I actually think that boxing is more dangerous because you can only punch during a boxing match. All you can do is punch the body and the head – but pretty much the head – that's where you get your knockout and that's where the brain damage comes from. At least if I'm getting hit I can wrestle a guy to the floor. I mean I wouldn't want to see boxing banned or anything like that – if two guys want to do that, it's up to them. If two guys want to punch each other continually in the face – great – but it's not for me. It's a bit brutal, I think. With what I do I can wrestle and I can beat a guy without hurting him and without him hurting me – I can get a submission or he'll tap out because he knows he's going to pass out, or his arm's going to pop or he's going to choke. I'll let it go then – it's fine, that's that.

'When I fight I'm a very good submission wrestler. My kick boxing's mediocre. I like to finish my fights on the mat, with a submission. That often means putting on a joint lock or a choke. If I put on a joint lock I'll do it so that the joint's ready to pop – like the elbow's going to come out, the shoulder's going to tear or the ankle's going to come out. Or else there's the choke, where the guy starts to pass out and he'll have to tap or he'll go straight to sleep. I mean it's not life threatening you know? If he does pass out they'll wake him up afterwards. But these guys had better tap before that happens, which they usually do, of course! They're not stupid. To get him there, onto the mat, is the thing. The guy doesn't just fall down for you. If I fight a kick boxer he's not going to want to wrestle, so you have to do what they call "closing the distance". Sometimes you punch your way in, to grab hold of the guy, or what I use a lot is something they call a "shoot" – you come out, dive onto your opponent with a good, calculated technique, avoiding the shots on the way in and you explode onto his legs, or onto his waist or round his shoulders and you take him down from there.'

Leigh's girlfriend Melinda has her own views about his love for no-holds-barred fighting. She told me, 'In general I feel that Leigh's fighting doesn't really bother me, until he actually goes abroad. Once he's gone I'm more nervous than he is. Leigh has won most of them as far as I know, so when he comes back he's all full of himself and it's all, "Aren't I wonderful." I think if he lost it would be a shock to him. It would bring him down to earth, really. He doesn't worry about it himself but I worry about him all the time, I worry even when he's training. If he comes back with a bruise or anything I want to know what happened and I want to make sure that every time he trains he's tapped them out and not the other way around. If they've tapped him out, I give him hell.

'On the build-up to a fight Leigh is training all the time and he just stays away. He doesn't stay at my house at all during the week before.

He may speak to me on the telephone but that's only if I push him. If it was up to him he'd not see me at all for the whole week beforehand and I'd just have to put up with it and wait until he got back.

'His aggression doesn't scare me, because he's not aggressive towards me and it's all directed towards his fighting. So it's no trouble to me at all.

'At the moment it's really important to him to go abroad because he feels that he's going nowhere in the UK and that he gets treated so much better outside. The money's so much better for a start and he would prefer to make it big abroad. America is, I think, his final goal. But he wants to be in the UFC, so if he makes it there he'll be happy.

'If Leigh works at his career in electronic engineering, I think he'll do far better money-wise than he would do in his fighting. As it stands at the moment I doubt the pay is going to match what he'll get once he's qualified. So to me, the money isn't in the fighting. I think it's more about an interest that he has.

'I don't mind him teaching our kids to fight if they want to learn to fight. At the moment the little one's far more interested than the big one. She'll shoot in and she'll get the choke or she'll punch him. In fact, Leigh had her attack me with the hammer the other day! If my little boy's naughty then Leigh gets my little girl to sort him out with head-butts and kicks. But if they're happy doing it then I guess I have to put up with it.'

TWELVE

SO LEIGH HAD DECIDED TO LEAVE THE DOMESTIC BLISS OF HOME and take a fight that he had found on the internet, in a country that he had never been to before, with promoters he did not know. He was being met there by a guy who he had not met before and had only spoken to twice on the phone. They had paid for his air ticket though, and for Leigh that was enough. As he touched down in Prague, Roman, his contact, was waiting for him.

Leigh told me later, 'I'm pretty tired but I'm glad I met Roman. I was a bit nervous as to whether anyone was going to be here for me – I came on my own and I'd never met anyone here. I'm feeling OK though and I'm ready to fight.'

'I've been told mainly by promoters that coming out here would be a bad idea. I don't know, maybe they fear the competition, or maybe they're genuinely worried for me that I'm going to get into trouble over here. I've been told that there is a lot of trouble – violence, a lot of crime. But that doesn't worry me, I'm just here to fight and go home again, I'm not here to live or anything. Still, it is a risk for me to come here – but I do feel I've outgrown the UK scene as it stands. Perhaps one day it'll improve, but to get the fights that I want I have to come abroad at the moment. It's good to fight in bigger shows, you know, and get more exposure. The quality of opponents available to me in the UK is a factor, but it's also just the size of the scene in general – the UK's very small so I have to move on. I've gone as far as I can in the UK and nothing's happening.

'I did actually quit fighting for a while, and then I did a few fights in the last programme and I got a lot of good response and it really took off again. So now I've got back into it, but I'd like to fight in the States in the UF scene. By fighting abroad, I think I'll be able to expand my horizons and it will give me the stepping stones that I need.

'A lot's happened recently: I've signed up with the Total Martial Arts, run by Ian Freeman and Julian Woodridge, who manage me – I haven't dropped Floyd Brown or anything, but these guys give me extra advice as well. So I've got it coming from both sides. They've set me up with a sponsor, Choke Athletic, for clothing – and it is good clothing, I'm not just saying that because they pay me! Also I've been doing a lot more training – it's stepped up now that I'm fighting professionally. I'm doing a lot more striking and wrestling too.

'The extra income that this stuff provides is pretty nice, it all helps. I really enjoy travelling and experiencing different cultures. It's just boring if, day in, day out, you just go up to London, go into the ring and fight some English guy and then leave again. It's nice when you first do it but I like to travel and this time in Prague is like a holiday for me.'

Roman originally knew as little about Leigh as Leigh knew about the Czech Republic. Roman told me, 'Well, I've since found out a lot about him. I know he's a very experienced fighter, so we're expecting a lot from him. The guy he's going to fight is a Thai boxer. He's had a couple of fights in Thai boxing and six Vale Tudo fights, with four wins and two losses.'

Roman had filled Leigh in on the rules of the Prague fight. Leigh told me, 'I was under the impression that if you fight in a ring, you have five rope escapes, when you can grab the bottom rope and the referee will break for you if you're in trouble. You can do that five times. I've just been informed by Roman, though, that we're fighting in a big cage, "the octagon". But I'm happy about that – I prefer it, being a submission fighter myself. It could work well for me.'

For those of you who don't know, 'the cage' is either a circular or octagonal construction. The Prague version measured about 18ft in diameter. Blue cloth covered the sprung flooring and underneath that, a network of scaffolding supported the whole structure. A 6½ft-high industrial-strength chicken-wire mesh enclosed the fighting area. The only way in or out was through a gate set into the perimeter fence. This set up is not particular to the Czech Republic – in the States it's called the octagon but in Brazil and most of the Eastern bloc countries it's known as the cage. Whatever it's called, it looks like a mini Roman amphitheatre minus the lions – and Leigh was one of the gladiators. In the Sky Sports Centre on the outskirts of Prague, Leigh started warming up for his Vale Tudo bare-knuckle fight.

The venue itself was not as you might imagine. It was an ordinary modern sports hall that had been converted for the evening's entertainment. A vast fighting area with a cage dominated the high vaulted hall. The Czechs had put on a real show. Outside the building a firework display was lit to start the proceedings and as crowds entered the sports hall they were greeted by the sight of dancing girls on top of two podiums on either side of the cage.

As the lights dimmed the dancing girls went to join more dancers inside the cage, the hall took on the feel of a nightclub hosting a cabaret. The girls – young, trim, athletic but slightly clumsy – stumbled their way through a dance routine. When they had finished the master of ceremonies made an announcement in Czech and introduced the fighters as they filed into the cage. Twelve of them, including Leigh, stood with their backs to the wire, facing the crowd. They were introduced one by one and when they had all been announced they left the cage in twos, opponents together, and headed back to the changing-room.

All the support staff were ready. The referee, dressed in a black short-sleeved shirt and black trousers, wore surgical gloves. The emergency medical staff, three green-uniformed nurses and a doctor, seemed equipped for World War III.

The early fights showed what Leigh could look forward to. Men returned to the changing-room with a range of injuries. The least of these belonged to a fighter whose nose was broken and whose eyes had turned black and purple after a well-aimed punch – and he was the winner of the fight! Another fighter came in boasting one bulging eye with all of its blood vessels burst. He had not tapped out quickly enough, and the choke hold had caused the damage. There were also broken knuckles and the usual bumps and bruises. One fighter came in with a cut above his eye that ran the length of his eyebrow. Czech rules about cuts are not very strict. In the UK fights are stopped almost immediately when a fighter is cut; it was, it seemed, very different here. In this case the referee had stopped the fight when he saw the cut, had dabbed it to stop it bleeding and then continued with the contest. Obviously his opponent then went straight for the eye and spread the cut. The fight was then stopped again. This time the doctor checked the guy, stitched him up within the allowed two minutes, and the bleeding stopped. The fight continued again. Again his opponent went for that eye. Eventually the fight was stopped a third time, the doctor examined the ever-widening chasm once again and this time the fight was pronounced over. Bare knuckle is brutal.

The changing-room soon began to look like an accident and emergency ward in a British hospital – the only difference being that here the patients were seen by a doctor quicker.

Leigh was next up. In his hooded Choke Athletic tracksuit he waited to be called into 'the cage'. The music boomed and he made his entrance to applause that was polite but loud. No-holds-barred fighters come in all shapes and sizes. All the ones I have seen have been tremendously fit and strong. Leigh is no exception – he is lean and there is not one ounce of fat on him. He has powerful arms and well-defined muscle definition, but his power really comes from his thighs. They are his pistons working to drive attacks. On this occasion Leigh was fighting a man who was the same weight but who looked thin and wiry.

The referee, in his rubber gloves, checked both fighters over for weapons. He returned to the centre and shouted at them in English.

'Are you ready?' he asked Leigh.

'Yes.'

'Are you ready?' the referee asked his opponent.

'Yes.'

They came to the centre of the cage and began to circle it and size each other up. Leigh immediately relaxed, his hands raised and his feet dancing. His opponent adopted a 'crouching tiger' pose – one hand shaped into a claw the other into a fist. Both men threw punches that missed, but they were more about shaking the other man's nerves that actually doing damage. One man threw a kick and the other stepped back; Leigh attacked with a combination, his opponent dodged it. Very little was coming Leigh's way and although no punch or kick had connected Leigh was coming up with ideas. He was on the attack. The circling continued; testing kicks and punches lashed out but they were always blocked or they just missed.

Then Leigh launched a real attack. He went as if to throw a punch but instead drove forward and low, grabbing the other man's legs and forcing him back onto the wire. The Czech managed to lift Leigh's arms so Leigh then grabbed the back of his neck, bending his head forward. At the same time Leigh brought his knee thudding up into the Czech's head. The Czech tried to move his head out of the way and Leigh immediately grabbed his waist, trying to get him onto the floor. The Czech clung onto the wire but Leigh was too strong and he had a firm grip on the Czech's waist. He used all his weight and with a judo-like throw he brought his man down, staying on top. This is exactly where Leigh wanted the fight to be – on the ground.

Leigh lay across the Czech, his full weight on him, his left hand pinning the man to the floor. Leigh's other hand was doing nothing, so noticing that the Czech's legs were open, Leigh punched him in the bollocks. Obviously this hurt the Czech who found himself suddenly charged with a new strength. He wriggled and squirmed to get out of Leigh's grip. He turned completely over, but Leigh still remained on top. Leigh was looking for a choke-hold around the other man's neck, or the opportunity to put him into one of his famous arm-bars. But his opponent knew he couldn't afford to let Leigh get away with anything. He hung onto the back of Leigh's neck.

In a move that galvanised the crowd into roars and gasps, Leigh sat up, his legs astride the other man's body and started pouring punches onto the Czech, driving them straight down into his head, right, left, right, left. The man bucked with his hips, throwing Leigh forward and at the same time he grabbed Leigh's neck again, pulling him in close. For a split second it worked. But Leigh was too strong – he pulled backwards and upwards, giving himself enough room to smash elbow shots down onto the top of the other man's head. The Czech pulled Leigh forward again and this time Leigh allowed himself to be pulled. With his forehead on the canvas he made a bridge with the rest of his body which gave him enough room underneath to swing punches into his opponent's body with both hands. The Czech bucked, trying to throw Leigh off but he stayed on. Leigh then saw his chance and went for the arm-bar, but he blew it. The Czech escaped, scrambling to his knees. Suddenly, out of the blue, the Czech was now on top. The crowd went wild.

Leigh stayed calm. He took two deep breaths and began to work his magic. He was not going to stay still for long. He hooked his feet under the Czech's legs and flipped him over. In a split second Leigh was on top again. Again he rained punches onto the Czech's head. They opened a cut on his cheek and blood soaked the canvas. The Czech wriggled again, trying to repeat his great escape but Leigh saw what was happening and changed his position to hold on. Soon he was able to get a choke-hold, cutting off the other man's oxygen supply. Frantically the Czech tried to escape. But it was for nothing – after a minute the Czech tapped Leigh's shoulder, indicating that he had given up. Leigh released the hold and stood up.

The doctor rushed in to examine the Czech, who eventually got up and we could see that the cut on his cheek was so big that it looked like another mouth. The two fighters shook hands and headed back to the changing-room while the referee mopped up the blood on the canvas and the dancing girls started to dance on their podiums again.

After the fight Leigh was high on adrenaline. 'He was really sweaty and when I went for an arm-lock he slipped out – he was so slippery he just slipped out of my hands – I was slipping everywhere. I went for the arm-bar too. But, he was quick as well, he was really, really wriggly, you know? My kick boxing could have been better I'm afraid. I didn't want to engage with him though because I couldn't kick with my shoes on. I threw one and I thought, they're going to penalise me. I came in – *wham*. But then I realised I had shoes on, so I decided not to again. He started kneeing me, so I went for the shoulders and the legs. I feel a little bit winded now actually, my head's burning a little bit. I think that's me getting a cold. I had a cold and a sore shoulder in there but I didn't want to say anything.

'He seemed very nice to me. To be honest though, I don't feel I've really met anyone that's an arsehole in the fight game, because they don't really have to prove anything. They're not in the street trying to frighten you or anything like that – you can actually just fight.'

The next day I caught up with Leigh at Prague airport as we waited for the flights back to the UK. The aches and pains of the night before had kicked in. Leigh said, 'I'm pretty tired – I had to get up pretty early to go to the airport. I'm a bit zonked right now. My hand's a bit sore from when I was hitting without a glove. I trained for fighting without gloves, though, so it wasn't as bad as it could have been. I trained hitting the bag with no gloves on, to condition my hands. But during the fight I caught my knuckle and it's a bit tender. I'm meant to be fighting this weekend again and I don't know if I'll be able to do it. Perhaps I'll be all right.'

Remembering the fight, Leigh told me, 'That guy's grappling wasn't too bad compared to UK standards, he was better than I thought he was going to be. He didn't really make any mistakes; I was just better than him, really. I expected more from him when we were on our feet.

He didn't want to trade with me – every time I came in to try and strike him, he'd back off and I wasn't even allowed to kick because I had shoes on. I didn't realise that I would be a better stand-up fighter than him – I wouldn't have worn the shoes if I'd realised. If I could have kicked him as well I definitely could have hurt him.

'The matting is very soft and so my shots were a bit slow and when he went to catch me I was worried about getting kneed and that. I've been there many times before. So I just drove into him and took him down. Since he was so slippery I knew I'd get the choke in, so in I went.

'I feel pretty good at this weight, I've lost some for this fight, but I'm still so much bigger and stronger than everyone else, it's a huge advantage. I've trained hard and mentally I'm strong too. I think maybe the schooling I do gives me mental discipline on top of everything else. Apparently this guy was an undefeated kick boxer, but that considered, he looked a bit crap on his feet to me. When we were standing up striking I expected a bit more from him. I'm not a great kick boxer but I was comfortable. In fact, I think he wanted to grapple with me really. Every time I came in to hit him, he backed away. But it was a really great fight. Fighting in that octagon was cool.

'Roman's been really cool about everything. He's been a really good ambassador for his country. The French fighters pulled out at the last minute, apparently, and I think a few English fighters did the same – so I don't think they're really going to be given the second chance to come out again. I don't think anyone's going to want to deal with those guys again. I think it was because there was a lot of confusion about how the tickets were going to be paid for, so guys were cautious about coming out here. I've been asked to bring some fighters out in the future though, and I think I'll do that. I think my fighters could do OK out here. I hope we can get something going.

'I thought the event itself was great – I didn't get to see all of it though, because I was getting prepared. But it looked really well run. I've been up to the UFC and this at least rivalled it in standard; it was really good. Other British fighters should come out here if they get the opportunity. The hospitality has been great. They treated me so well, like a real fighter. My hotel cost was totally covered; my flight's totally covered; I haven't spent any money at all since I've been here either – I've been taken out three times a day. My entertainment's all been covered. They've treated me really, really well.

'From what I've seen I think the culture out here is similar to the UK. The language is obviously different, but the way things are done is closer to the UK than it is to the States. It's very similar to home. In fact, I don't really feel that I'm in a foreign country or anything. The people here are just the same, they're pleasant.

'I came out here on my own because there is only one round in these fights, so a corner-man wasn't really essential to me. I didn't really need a coach or anything either and, without wanting to put anyone down, I don't think they have as much money over here as we do in the West, so I thought if I could save them the price of a plane ticket, or whatever, that would be cool. It was a bit nerve-wracking coming out here on my own though, I was hoping I wouldn't get stuck, I didn't really have a clue where I was going – people were telling me I was going to be stuck in some Eastern bloc country, with armed policemen dragging me everywhere but now I've been over here, it's not anything like that – it's a great country and the people are really hospitable.

'I think people need to be educated towards this kind of fighting. People might seem intelligent but they can be idiots, you know? They'll go, "Oh, look at that thuggery." People just don't appreciate the skill involved. Look at boxing – it's just punching someone in the face – that's it – for 12 rounds. *That* is thuggery. If they want to do it, fair enough. But as far as the public is concerned, they don't appreciate that, especially in England where boxing's almost a tradition. And they don't appreciate the skill involved in what we do. So many people think that their martial-art style that they're trained in is so good it's going to beat everyone and I've proved that it doesn't. That's what I like about this sport; you can prove what styles really work. The less rules you have in a fight the closer it is to a real one.

Some people like boxing, so having rules is better for them. But our fighting is better if you want to see how a real fight works.

'A mate of mine was in a bar and he got into a fight – it didn't last more than five seconds before he popped this other guy's arm out. These guys in "real" fights don't train. That's down to them, if they don't want to train that's fair enough. But I don't want to fight untrained fighters. I want to fight skilful guys, guys that are trained in their discipline.

'I don't think there's anyone really under 80 kilos who can challenge me. I'm down to 68 or 69 right now; I've lost a lot of weight. And still there's no one who can touch me, probably even under 70 kilos. I don't want to sound like I'm bragging and I don't want to put anyone else down, but the truth is I've got so much more experience than anyone else that once I get in that ring they can't compete with me.

'I'm in my final year of my studies – I got a first last year, which was a surprise to me. I'd like to do it again this year, a repeat performance. So I'm going to knuckle down a lot with my studies. I don't know how much I'll be travelling. I've signed, apparently, to fight in Japan, and America want me to come out again and fight in the UFC. We'll have to see what happens.

'I teach fighting twice a week and I get some training in then too, with the fighters. I do judo once a week and I kick box when I've been getting the chance recently. I lift weights three times a week and I run too. Floyd Brown's got me doing all this training. It's really good, it's made a big difference. I couldn't believe how hard I was hitting yesterday. I gave him a couple of shots and it just smashed him right up. The average total time I spend is about five times a week, training for fighting.

'I'm lucky; I've got a skill. Maybe I've grown up learning it, or maybe it's innate, but I can switch into fight mode instantaneously. I can be really passive and calm one moment, joking around, and then I get into the ring or get into the cage and something changes and I'm ready to fight, I'll get really wound up.

'I'd definitely come back here. I'm hoping to, actually. We spoke to some of the guys here and they've asked me to come back and they want me to bring some other guys as well. If I can bring some other fighters out that would be cool. Perhaps that could happen next March. I'm supposed to be fighting Jeremy Bailey in the UK then. But, to be honest, they'd have to offer me something these guys couldn't. This set-up is so good. I would like to fight Jeremy though. There's a lot of talk about it. I don't want to put the guy down, but I really don't think he's in my league. He's a very good kick boxer, but as far as no holds barred goes, he's nothing compared to me. I want to fight him, but if they want to see a fight, they'll have to offer me something substantial because I'd rather fight here.

'I've moved in with my girlfriend now and at the moment fighting comes first. She's a very nice girl, but from the beginning, I've always said that fighting comes first. I love it; it's what I do. She whinges a bit about the fact that I spend so much time training. She wasn't happy about me coming out here either – she'd heard a lot of bad stuff about the place. She hasn't seen me fight live yet – she'd have come out here but she wasn't happy about that idea.'

The organisation that put on the event in Prague was keen to attract other fighters from the UK and their representative, Roman, had this as a clear objective. He told me: 'As the manager for foreign relations, I take care of the foreign fighters when they come in, but I also try to promote all fighters and get them out to foreign countries to fight.

'I'm really the middleman between the Czech Ultimate Fighting Association and the promoters. The association has been around for about three years. We've had 11 tournaments altogether. This will be our fifth this year and it will actually be the second time we have had foreign fighters coming in. We have Leigh and we have German fighters too. I put out some ads on internet pages and they just contacted me. Leigh seemed very interested in fighting in our event and it seemed like the right type of event for him. He loved the rules and I think that's the main reason he came over. A lot of people have the wrong idea about this country; they still think it is the place it was ten years ago. But a lot has changed. I think there are less rules over here in fighting than there are in England and some other places; it's more like Brazil here. They're real Vale Tudo fights here – 20-minute rounds, with 5 minutes of overtime. They're in cages, with no gloves. The only illegal techniques are eye-gouging, fish hooking, open-hand strikes to the ears and biting. [Fish-hooking is a move that is not allowed any more in mixed martial arts events in this country as it can cause horrendous damage to the face, literally ripping it apart. The hooked finger is forced into the fleshy corner of your opponent's mouth, like a fish caught by a hook, and the finger is ripped back fast.] Everything else is allowed. Vale Tudo is getting popular here. We're also doing Thai boxing fights now, which are more popular, but I think Vale Tudo fights are the future. We get between 1,500 and 2,000 people at our events. The biggest one we had was over 4,000 people.

'We had some more foreign fighters that were supposed to come in to this tournament but they backed out as they were afraid and they didn't know what to expect. Leigh was the only one who stepped up and took the challenge like a true warrior. We need more foreign fighters to take part. We want fighters from all around the world to come in, but so far not many are willing to risk it, I guess. Our fights are videotaped and they are televised. There was a half-hour show that would cover the event, involving Thai boxing and Vale Tudo fights.'

So Leigh left the Czech republic still undefeated. He had fought in a cage bare knuckled and survived. In Prague they liked their Vale Tudo raw and bloody with few rules but there are places around the world where there are even fewer rules, if you can imagine that . . .

Another fighting tradition that is older than the hills is Irish bare-knuckle fighting. In Ireland it is still done in the old-fashioned way. We found it to be an underground pursuit, but still very much alive.

THIRTEEN

BARE-KNUCKLE FIGHTS TAKE PLACE ANYWHERE FROM FIELDS AND country lanes, to travellers' sites, farmyards and the back of car parks – they'll hold them anywhere big enough to hold two men and a crowd. We found several going on in Ireland, but the one described here seemed a good example of how it all happens and gives a real sense of what it is like – just as it was 100 years ago. Some names of the people in this chapter have been changed to preserve anonymity.

Tommy bandaged Mick's hands in silence. Mick sat on the passenger seat of the Ford Mondeo, his shirt off, as Tommy crouched in front of him working quickly, winding the yellowing blood-stained dressing around the giant, thick hands. You could see that his knuckles had been pushed back, broken or smashed to virtually nothing from previous battles. By the end of the day the few that were left would break again against the bone of the other man's skull. Looking over Tommy's broad, heavy back and shoulders, Mick kept his eye on the crowd pushing and shoving around the car. Every now and then he gave instructions to Tommy to tighten the bandage.

The passenger door of the car was open in such a way that it protected the fighter and his second from any would-be attackers. It was not unknown for a man with a claw hammer or a screwdriver to appear from the crowd and smash the fighter over the head with it. Someone who had bet on Mick's opponent, for instance, may want to knobble Mick before the fight.

There were between 25 and 30 men crammed into this part of the narrow country lane that ran next to a bypass. On the other side of the hedge, some distance away, cars sped past, their drivers rushing to work, taking kids to school or on their way to Sainsburys to do some early-morning shopping. Articulated lorries rushed to deliver food and consumer durables to shops in nearby towns. They had no idea that beyond the verge and behind the hedge and brambles a bare-knuckle fight was about to start.

In the narrow, crowded country lane the atmosphere was building. The shouts and swearing from the crowd made the place sound almost like a capacity crowd at Premier League football match at the moment just before the home team come onto the pitch – except that the language was southern Irish, a blend of Gaelic and Irish gypsy traveller slang. Virtually nothing was understandable to an English ear.

Cash was being thrust into the hand of a short, fat, middle-aged, grey-haired man sitting on the bonnet of the car. He was wearing a leather pork-pie hat that was too small for him, sported at a tilt on his fat head. Every now and then someone appeared from the crowd and thrust money at him. It was counted, the payer's name was noted down, and the money was placed in a black Adidas holdall that was already filled to capacity. The bag was guarded by a short, trim man dressed in a black vest and khaki trousers. There must have been over fifty thousand in cash in that bag and with a crowd like this you never know who might want to try and take it before the fight was over.

Tommy had finished bandaging Mick's hands. He took a deep breath, filling his lungs, and stood up. The car's suspension moaned and slowly returned to it's normal position as Mick's weight lifted. It was remarkable now to see Mick towering above everyone else in the crowd. All 6ft 4in of him uncoiled. He strode through the crowd like a grown-up walking through a playground of children. He was not muscular in the same way that bodybuilders are, trim and well defined. A thick layer of skin covered Mick's rock-hard, smooth muscles. His shoulders, arms, chest and neck where solid and large but his arms were loose and flexible. He was built more like Ali than Foreman. Close-up you could see several long, purple scars on his torso and back. These knife scars were deep and neat and were the legacy of a thousand other battles fought in fields, caravan sites and back rooms of clubs and pubs. Stabbing him was probably the only way you could stop Mick, and even then you had to avoid those long, powerful arms and fists like jackhammers. It was doubtful if the men who had stabbed him had managed to get away with it unharmed. The phrase 'you should have seen the other fella' sprung to mind.

For a split second, as the crowd took in his size they were silent. Only the roar of the traffic on the bypass could be heard from people there oblivious to the tension in the lane. Everyone looked in awe at the size and power of this man. Then, just as suddenly, everyone snapped out of their trances and started where they had left off, talking at a hundred miles an hour.

Testosterone pulsed through the crowd at a faster rate now, in anticipation of the fight to come. They pushed and shoved each other, cursed and swore. Small skirmishes erupted at the edges of the crowd. Punches, kicks and head-butts were traded. In blood-spattered clothes, the fighters were separated by fathers, brothers or uncles, only to kick off again somewhere else in the crowd. All this was going on around Mick who watched for any attackers coming for him. He swatted men away from him when, by mistake, they were pushed or punched into his path. Tommy was there ahead of him, cutting a swathe through the crowd and keeping everyone well away from his boy. Mick lifted his head and looked beyond the crowd to the top of the lane and stopped. He had seen what nobody else had been able to. Coming towards him, with another small crowd around him, was the man he was about to fight.

Fifty metres away, another Irish traveller emerged from the centre of his crowd of supporters. Short, squat and square, he looked like he was carved out of a single block of granite. With dark, cropped hair and grey, slate-like eyes he looked younger than Mick, around 26, and much shorter too – but his power was unmistakable. They called him 'The Bull' and he was a bull terrier of a man. He moved quickly with short, sharp steps. He had a thick, fat waist and neck and this, combined with his low centre of gravity, made him an almost immovable force. Tommy was even now sizing him up, working out a strategy.

The Bull broke free from his supporters and advanced to the spot where Tommy was waiting. He looked around, surveying the narrow lane, seeing if there was enough room for the men to fight. He took a deep breath and very theatrically ripped off his shirt. His buttons popped off and flew in all directions. There was a low groan from the crowd as they saw the mauve scar that ran from the left side of his chest, just under his collarbone, down over his stomach and continuing down past the top of his jogging bottoms. The holes from the stitches that must have effectively held his organs in had healed but were still clearly visible. He whispered something into his second's ear. The man approached Mick and they shook hands.

The two sets of supporters formed a ring around the two fighters and the seconds. A fifth man joined them in the centre. He was 'the best man' and would act as a referee, deciding who won the fight. It would not be Queensbury rules and this man certainly did not wear the obligatory white shirt and black tie typical of boxing referees. Instead he wore a bright yellow-and-red Hawaiian short-sleeved shirt, and trousers from a '70s dinner suit over working boots.

The best man brought the two fighters together and the seconds fell back. A small child held her father's hand at the front of the ring of supporters. She looked as though she was in the front row of the audience at a circus, waiting for the clowns to come. All that was missing was her ice cream and a balloon on a string.

Both fighters shook hands and immediately The Bull stepped back, expecting a blow from Mick but it didn't come. The rules were shouted out for all to hear so that there could be no arguments afterwards. The fighters were ordered to start and the fight was on.

Instantly, The Bull charged at Mick; he came in low and with a combination of fast, wide hooks to his head. Mick took a step back and raised his arms which soaked up the punches. Sensing that Mick was on the back foot, The Bull let fly another volley of fast hooks. This time Mick stood his ground and kept his arms high, twisted his upper body and used The Bull's momentum to send him flying into the crowd behind him. Men fell backwards into the brambles behind him, but they pushed The Bull back into the fighting zone. But while he was being thrown backwards he had automatically turned to stop himself falling – a huge mistake. Now he had his back to Mick and he was off balance. Mick moved in and clubbed him with the edge of his fist, on the top of his head – careful not to damage his own knuckles on the head of the other man. He followed it up with an elbow, which came down vertically on the top of The Bull's neck. The best man stepped in and separated the fighters. For a moment it looked as if The Bull was out of it; he looked dazed and wobbled unsteadily on his feet. Mick's supporters sensed victory and The Bull's men watched his every move and shouted half-hearted encouragement. It looked to be over almost before it had started.

The two men moved back into the middle of the gravel lane and faced each other. The Bull shook his head to clear the fog and then to everyone's surprise he raced in while Mick's guard was down. He had apparently faked his injury. He had wanted to get close to Mick and do damage at short range, thereby avoiding Mick's long reach. It worked. Mick was shocked. Two short, thunderous hooks – left and right – caught him on the jaw. Mick took a step back, moving his head out of reach of the smaller man who was now throwing blows up at Mick, but this time he was missing. Instantly, Mick let loose a left jab that shot out from his shoulder. It looked innocent, nothing really to worry about, apparently involving hardly any effort – but the power came in the last split second as it hit its target. The noise was sickening, a cross between a slap and a thud. The image of a large carcass on a butcher's hook being punched with a bare fist popped into mind.

Some small bones in Mick's hand had broken. The Bull's eyebrow burst open, spurting blood a full metre into the air. Mick followed this up with a short right hook. The fist glanced off The Bull's nose and it was followed by Mick's elbow coming crashing in, a split second behind it, smacking into The Bull's jaw.

The smaller man was reeling. If he'd faked injury before, he wasn't faking now. Miraculously though, his legs held. He was not out yet, but he was in trouble. The Bull grabbed hold of the big man, clinging on for dear life, holding those powerful arms down to prevent more damage being done. But he knew he could not hold on for long. In desperation he bit down as hard as he could into Mick's fleshy shoulder, just below the neck. Still Mick did not push him away. He had freed up his right hand and was winding up for a big punch. The best man had seen the bite, which was against the rules. He stepped in and separated the two men. He warned them again that biting was strictly forbidden. Mick complained bitterly. As he wiped the blood away, a perfect print of The Bull's teeth could be seen clearly on the left side of his broad shoulders. The Bull's eye was bleeding. A blood-and-snot number 11 streamed under his nose. The best man again called the fighters together.

Mick's anger burned in his eyes but he held on to it. He did not release the rage. Blood covered the smaller man's face on the left side, but it did not interfere with his vision. Again and again The Bull charged and every time Mick stuck out the jab like a piston, aiming for and finding the split eye. Every time it hit 'oooh's and 'ahhh's went up from the crowd. Now both men were covered in blood. But The Bull kept going, mostly missing with shots to Mick's head. This is what they call 'game' – a man moving forward, ignoring pain and risking ever more damage to himself.

In a natural break in the fight (there were no rounds) the best man stepped in. He looked at The Bull's eye and asked him if he wanted to go on. He nodded. His face was now completely deformed. The damaged eye was just visible under the swelling, which spread down the whole side of his face. He pulled the corner of his mouth up in a grotesque, lopsided smile. Fluid had built up under the soft tissue of his face and it looked ready to burst through the skin. It surely wouldn't be able to take much more, even if The Bull could.

To cheers of the crowd the entertainment continued. Mick's bandages were coming undone and his hands were broken. He wanted to keep on attacking The Bull's eye but contact with the bone was just too damaging to his own hands. He switched to punching The Bull's chest, just over his heart, and also with direct hits to his stomach – the 'bread bin'. It worked. The Bull was forced back up the lane, from where he had come. The crowd moved up, the fighters in the centre. The Bull and Mick looked as if they had an invisible forcefield around them, a halo of space, inside which only the high priest, the best man, was allowed.

The end, when it came, was not spectacular. It was not a knockout, or some massive right cross, knocking The Bull off his feet and flat onto his back. The Bull did not make a last-minute comeback and beat Mick in some Irish-traveller version of David and Goliath. In the end Mick was just too strong and big for The Bull, who had probably wanted to go on, even if it meant until he died. But the truth is that he simply ran out of puff. The massive hits that Mick was putting in, together with the damage to The Bull's eye and those blows to his chest, sapped his strength and winded him. As Mick wound up for another bone-shaking right punch, The Bull held up his hand and surrendered. It was over.

The fighters shook hands and their supporters drifted away. The men who had bet on Mick returned to his car to collect their winnings from the Adidas bag. Mick went back there too to get his prize money.

Tommy unwound the blood-stained bandages and a tooth fell out. The man who'd been holding the little girl's hand was now holding her up in his arms. He gave Mick a pen and he signed one dressing and gave it to the little girl, who hid her face in her father's neck so her father took them, with a nod and wink to Mick. Mick gave the other bandage to the man in the pork pie hat, who counted eighteen thousand pounds out of the holdall at the speed of light and handed it to Mick.

Mick's breathless speech to the camera was spoken in English. 'He was a good, strong man and it was a good fight. I want to thank Tommy and all those who helped me, and also everyone who helped put up the eighteen-thousand-pound prize money.' He put on his shirt, got into his car and then he and Tommy drove up the lane and turned towards the bypass. The car tilted at a strange angle, the suspension once again straining under Mick's weight. The top of his head must have been pushing through the lining of the car's roof too. His huge shoulders were wider than the seat. The difference in size between Tommy and Mick was so huge it was comical – but no one dared laugh.

Ireland is still a place were you can see a bare-knuckle fight if you know where to look and who to ask. The people involved don't much like outsiders, especially those with cameras; it is a closed society. They continue to fight in the way they have done for centuries and it will carry on in country lanes, fields, caravan sites and waste ground – or right next to the roads and motorways you may be using to get to work. What we had seen was brutal, barbaric and basic but somehow it was also honest and honourable. Everyone there seemed to accept it as normal.

FOURTEEN

TO FIND OUT MORE ABOUT THIS CULTURE I TURNED TO SOMEONE who grew up in it. For travellers, fighting for family honour or for money is not unusual or frowned upon. Bobby Frankham grew up in the travellers' community and his family are legendary in it. When Brad Pitt was researching his character as a gypsy bare-knuckle fighter in Guy Ritchie's film *Snatch* he also turned to Bobby for help. One weekend Brad flew in from LA to stay with Bobby at his home. Bobby gave him a crash course in the gypsy language and fighting bare knuckle. Brad's character traits are based on that weekend spent with Bobby Frankham – Bobby's still got the Polaroids to prove it.

Bobby himself has both seen and fought in many bare-knuckle battles. He says, 'I grew up in Newmarket in Suffolk. My dad loved horse racing, so that's where we stayed. We bought a bit of land and built a big house there where we all lived. My dad was a man called Johnny Frankham. He was the best man I've ever known, to tell you the truth. He took us everywhere with his boxing. When I was eight we used to follow "Gypsy Johnny Frankham". I wanted to get into a boxing club when I was nine – I was like a little tearaway at that age, but they only took you from the age of eleven, so I bumped my age up by two years 'cos I was so keen to get in. So I ended up fighting boys two years older than me. I was winning some and losing some bouts but when I was thirteen I had to tell them the truth because by then I was boxing guys who were almost men, with beards, and I still had a baby face. So when I told them the truth they put me back two years and I started to win all my fights. I started doing well. I won every competition. I entered ABA's [Amatuer Boxing Association fights] and I went to Germany and won there so it was good. I actually got banned as an amateur at a club called Brookside in Watford.

'My dad trained us – he loved boxing and so we loved boxing. We weren't forced to box, we wanted to, to make him proud of us. That's all we wanted to do. He used wake us up in the morning and take us running. Or he'd come in from work and take us training. Sometimes if we were travelling around in the summer in the trailers and going to the gym meant turning back 50 miles, we'd do it. He wouldn't only take us; if anyone else was around he would take them as well, he'd go, "You wanna go, boys?" He was dedicated to us and he loved boxing.

'There's loads of different kinds of gypsies – some do live on the side of the road and they look scruffy, not caring where they live. It's the same in your culture: there are people who live in council houses, people who own their own council houses and there are some who live in mansions. Well, you get poor gypsies, wealthy ones, scruffy ones and smart ones. It's the same in every race – you get yer good and yer bad. Often you only see the bad gypsies. We're the good ones though and we pay our taxes.'

For Bobby, fighting in the boxing ring was part of growing up. But what about the illegal bare-knuckle fighting, where did he see that for the first time?

'When we were little and I was in a pram, we used go to gypsy fairs. When I was five or six years old I was old enough to see a fight. Sometimes when you go to a fair you'd get word that there was going to be a fight that day. People would come to watch it. But in those days it was pretty safe, you could watch it as a kid. The two men would have their shirts off and they would have a fight but they would fight fair. There would be no head-butting and no kicking. If a man went down he went down and if he didn't want to carry on he wouldn't – it would be finished. Then they would get up and go and have a drink – unless he'd had all his teeth knocked out, then he wouldn't – but that's what it was like in them days. It's more violent there these days.

'I decided I wanted to be a boxer. Sometimes when I went to a fair there would be the odd cheeky man who wanted to fight me, or there would be a so-and-so who was coming from Ireland who thought he was a bit useful. But to be truthful I didn't want to do it, I thought, what's the point? I wanted to do it in the boxing ring, properly. If the Boxing Board of Control had been fair with me I would have been a champion. But they weren't and I've got to live with that.' Bobby lost his boxing licence as a professional fighter when a decision went against him; he complained and in the scuffle that followed the referee was manhandled.

'There are thousands of gypsies all over the place – England, Scotland, Wales, everywhere. In Cambridge, there's a fair that had been going on for donkey's years. It's right in the middle of town and the travellers used to stop in the fields behind, just about a mile from it. But the council stopped them coming. They said it was too much for the town. So all the young kids and old people come down now just for the one day, instead of the week they used to come for. They used to come down in their trailers from all over the place, and all live there peacefully, until things got bad. There used to be fights back then too, but they would be arranged fights.

'Old gypsies like a bit of spinning the coins. They have a ring made up for it, where they all gamble. When they're on the camps they want something to do, apart from drink and chat. So they would gamble. Some of them would wait all year round, saving their money for it. But if there's any fights on, on the Saturday of the fair, the main day, everyone's there, and they fight in that ring.

'I saw my brother fight there once, over a woman who is now his wife. But someone tried to take the piss out of him, and he wouldn't stand for it. 'Cos my brother – he could fight. He was tough. And he just wasn't going to stand for it. At the time he had a broken hand. He'd just had a professional fight where he'd broken it. He'd just won the ABA's in London. He still wanted to fight, but he was walking around Cambridge with a broken hand. And this fellow, a big guy, tried to take the piss out of him, trying to say something about his girl. Anyway they got arguing over it and he said, "All right, just 'cos I got one hand, don't think that I'm afraid of you – I'll fight you. Tomorrow morning, in the ring at the fair."

'The next morning he was up at 7 a.m. A lot of people didn't hear about the fight that day 'cos the argument had happened late at night. But we knew all about it. That morning he got his scissors and cut the plaster straight off his hand. Then they had the fight. It only lasted a couple of seconds – my brother come in and *bang, bang*, he hit him on the chin. He just put him down – no kicking, nothing like that. He knocked him down. The fellow got up and said, "All right I'm sorry, fair enough, fair play." They shook hands and that was how it was left. In fact, they are mates now, have been ever since. The guy got beaten fair and square. That's the way gypsies used to organise their fights. It's changed with time though, I think.

'I've had a few fights in nightclubs and whatever, but I've not been one to go and take the piss. There's no marks on my face at all. I don't really like fighting. But if someone's done something that was totally taking liberties or whatever . . . I'd stick up for someone, you know what I mean? If someone was being bullied I'd always be the one to say, "Hold on, mate." Once, in my younger days, I was in this pub in Newmarket, and there was an old boy, and he was going around picking up glasses. He was getting probably a couple of quid a night and he was a little bit backward. But he was a real nice old boy. He went to pick an empty glass up from a hard man in the pub one day, a guy everyone was terrified of. He picked this glass up, and this man, he just hit this old boy, knocked him onto the floor, then picked him up and hit him again – for nothing. And he knew this guy was backward as well. But no one stuck up for him 'cos they were terrified of this man. He was a big, hard ginger bastard, to tell you the truth. Anyway, I went and stuck up for him. I said, "Hold on, mate. Leave it out. He's a bit backward. You shouldn't do that." He said, "Why, are you gonna help him? Do you wanna help him?" I said, "No, mate, I don't wanna help him." Anyway, he kept on and on and eventually I said, "Look, mate, I don't fight in pubs but if you wanna come outside I'll fight you." So out he came. He didn't even know how to put his hands up. He put his hands up like a woman. I just went straight through him – *bang, bang* – I hit him a couple of times I think. I broke his cheekbone and his jaw with two hits. People came out the pub and they applauded me. I felt bad, but he'd done a bad thing, hitting a backward boy in a pub. That's the sort of person I was. No one in the pub would do it 'cos they were terrified of this man who was the big hard-man of Newmarket at the time. I was only a young boy then, about 17 or 18. I just took him out there and hit him a couple of times. I wasn't scared – I didn't care how big or small he was – unless he had a big sawn-off shotgun, and then I'd have run and come back another day!

'I've had a couple of fights at fairs. I went to one at Epsom Races with some good Irish friends of mine I'd known all my life called the Dohertys, who used to live about two miles from my house. I was 18 years old, I think. But I didn't go to get into trouble or anything. I went there to have a good day, to have a gamble as usual; to have a good bet, and a good spin of the coins, and to try and win a few quid. There always used to be parties there for the travellers. Anyway, I'm going to the fair with the two Doherty brothers. When we get to the races they told me they were gonna have a fight. He looks at me and says, "Listen, we're having a fight but it ain't gonna be fair. Can you watch my back for me? We're gonna get on the floor, we're gonna gouge each other's eyes out, we're gonna bite each other, we're gonna rip each other, we're gonna fight till we die, till it finishes. That's how it's gonna be. And what I want you to do is just watch me back." I was easy led back then, you know what I mean? So I said I'd do it. What I didn't realise was that there were going to be 500 travellers there, about 10 English and the rest Irish – all over the place, screaming and going mad. But I still stuck by my mate. Even though there were so many people there – he was my mate and I was going to stick by him like I said I would.

'So it came to the fight and he was fighting on the floor. It wasn't fair or nice to watch, to tell you the truth. I ain't into all that, I like a bit of fair fighting. I like it held in the ring, too, to tell you the truth. But everyone knew it was going to be like that. There was no one else joining in or anything, but they were on the floor, biting and ripping and doing whatever. My mate's giving his opponent a right good beating, he's ripping bits off him. He's biting his ears and ripping his face – honestly it's not nice to watch. And suddenly this fellow comes over and – *crack*, he hits my mate in the middle of the fight. So I've gotta help him now, ain't I? And with that – *bam, bam* – I've hit this fellow.

'He was a guy called Bimi Ward. He was a professional boxer at the time, a fighting fellow. Anyway, I hit him a couple of times, I think. The fight was stopped. I was glad it did stop in a way because I didn't want it to get as bad as it was getting. I didn't think any more of it, I was only 18 at the time.

'Three years later I stopped boxing amateur, I just lost a little bit of interest. I thought, I've won everything – I won the schoolboys' and the ABA's – which I thought was going to be a big thing, but I only got little medals. When I was young, I thought winning that kind of thing was gonna be good. But it was a disappointment. Since I was a gypsy they didn't wanna pick me to box for England either. It was just the way it was: they thought we gypsies were too rough, but we were good fighters.

'Anyway, I packed up boxing after that. I thought, I'll go out and try a little bit of this drinking business, 'cos I'd never drunk. I thought, I'm gonna start smoking a few fags, make myself a man – I'm young and I'm gonna do what all the other boys do: go out with all the girls and have myself a good time, that kind of thing. I decided to hang my gloves up, I'd had enough of it. I'd boxed since I was nine years old, and now I was eighteen or nineteen – it's a long time really. And anyway, I still knew how to hold my hands up and defend myself. And I wasn't frightened of any man; I'd fight anyone if I had to if there was a good enough reason. I wouldn't just say "Rip your shirt off and fight." I don't wanna just fight for the sake of it. If a man hit me, then I would retaliate, that's the way I am.

'If I could get away with not fighting, I would. Ideally I wouldn't go anywhere with lots of other gypsies – only my own family. I wouldn't go to gypsy fairs 'cos you usually get some little fool there who thinks he's a man for a day, with a few lagers in him. He'd rip his shirt off and he'd soon get put on his arse. I packed that kind of thing up. I decided to go out with the boys. I did that for three or four years and my weight went up from about eleven stone to about eighteen stone. It wasn't so much the beer, it was more just eating and not training – and just going out and enjoying myself.

'Some time later I decided to go to the Epsom Races again for the day with a friend of mine, Les. He was a very good friend of the family too. He's Irish and a bit of a traveller. We decided to go to the Races for pleasure, to have a few bets and whatever. I wasn't even gonna go to the spinning ring, to tell you the truth, where all the travellers meet. I thought I'd just mix with all the gorgers [non-gypsies] round the stands. Anyway, I got there, made a huge bet on the horses and lost the lot. So I thought I'd better go around to the travellers to borrow a few quid off someone. I bumped into one of the boys and borrowed £100 off him.

'Later, I'm off with Les having a spin of the coins, enjoying myself. Thousands of people are there. I wasn't thinking about fighting at all at that time, it never entered my mind. I hadn't been in trouble for ages. I hadn't come for a fight. Besides, I'm about 17 or 18st, a little porker. The next thing I know, I hear that Bimi Ward's there – the man I hit when I was 18. I suppose he never forgot about it. If I could possibly have disappeared, I would have. I thought, I don't need this. I don't wanna fight, really. All my mates were there, I wasn't gonna back down from him, but I really didn't want it. I guess the fellow was entitled to come and give me another challenge from that time four or five years ago. But I had no idea he was gonna be there. If I'd known I wouldn't have gone, it's as simple as that. Anyway, they told me that Bimi Ward was on his way, that he'd be there in ten minutes, he was up at Tattenham Corner, already walking down. I thought – nice. I looked over to my mates and said, "Boys, I ain't had no training, I ain't trained for about a year. I've been out with you dossers, clubbing it and pubbing it, I've even started smoking 20 fags a day." I said, "I've never been beaten in my life and this is the day you're gonna see me get a good hiding. Look at him." He was like a machine coming down there towards me. Anyway when he arrives he tells me he wants a fight in the betting ring. I told him I wouldn't. Three or four years before I would have done if I'd been the same weight as him. But I was a slob to him by now. He had the whole of that time since I'd hit him to get himself ready for me. And he had done as well, 'cos he was as fit as a fiddle. He wasn't as tall as me but he was fit and he was a professional boxer at that time – he'd had a few good fights, he'd won a few of them and he had a big following. I told him I'd fight him outside the ring. He had a lot of Irish people with him – perhaps about five or six hundred – all there to cheer him on. They were behaving well, but only because I had a lot of English people there with me – good people, the best of the best.

'There was a guy called Boxer's Tom, a good man, quite a small fellow. There was another fellow called John Stanley, and I had Les Stephens too, who fought John Conti for the Light Heavyweight Championship of Europe. He's my cousin. I had Gypsy John there too – there were loads of them there all watching.

'You could see Bimi Ward coming towards us, training shoes on, shirt off and there was a crowd following him. And there I am in a pair of old trousers, as fat as a pig with a pair of boots on. I said to my mate, "Lend me your trainers," and I put them on. I told Bimi that I wanted to fight in the field, so we fought in the middle of the trailer field there, just as the Derby was finishing. It took nearly an hour altogether with a break halfway through.

'We made this big ring and the fight started. It was frightening because there were a lot of drunken people there, there were police on horses, there were lords and ladies in the race stand who'd been watching the Derby and started watching the fight through binoculars with their top hats and tails on. They were cheering and chanting, and that's God's honest truth. I was told afterwards that policemen were even taking bets on us.

'So the fight starts. I thought, this fellow's so fit he's gonna come straight in and beat the arse right off me 'cos I ain't fit. But I was still tough, and I was very, very skilful. I could read a man. When a man throws a punch I can see it coming from his eyes, when he flings it I can read the move. I was good. The field where we were fighting was on a bit of a bank. So I stood on the high bit so he had to come upwards towards me, so I had the advantage there. Plus, he was smaller than me so I had advantage there too. I could jab at him and every time he came at me I could just lean back and he'd miss me a lot of the time.

'I thought, if I try and go in towards him I might lose my breath if I don't knock him out – 'cos he's Irish and tough. He was a gladiator; he wanted a fight. He had got all his family there – he wanted a fight to the death. He would have fought me to the death, too. It's as simple as that. This time round he was the toughest man I've ever fought in my life. In the ring or out of the ring this man could fight now. Anyway, I thought I'd take one on the chest, just to see if he could hit hard. I thought that if he couldn't hit hard, and I took it on the chest, I would go in and try and do what I did when I fought him before. I'd just hit him a couple of times and he'd just go down and the fight would be over. But of course I was fit back then.

'So I'm boxing properly, and I knew I had plenty of time. I wasn't panicking; I never panic. Every time he came in I was just out-boxing him, *bang, bang*. He flings this jab at me and then comes in with his big right. I'm ready to take it on the chest like I'd planned, all tensed up 'cos I know it's coming. As I'm ready to take it on the chest my foot slips down a horse hole, where the horses have been tied up in the field. I slipped down and he hit me right in the mouth. Full smack – *smash*. He's buckled me. I didn't go right down but my hand hit the ground. I bounced back up, but when he hit me he got me full in the front teeth and I could feel them wobble, all loose. The blood was squirting everywhere. My nose was bust too. My eyes were fine, but he'd hit me full in the mouth.

'But hitting me in the mouth wasn't much good for him because if you're a street fighter you never hit someone in the mouth, if you do you're gonna smash your hand to pieces straight away. So you try to hit him on the side of the face, with a hook or whatever – you're far better off doing that. Anyway, he hit me in the mouth and bust it all up and when I bounced back up I said, "Good shot!" I more or less laughed at him. Then I put my hands back up and I was serious again. I thought, OK, he hits hard, but I ain't gonna go in and try and bust him. I'll just play with him. So I fought on for 30 minutes. Every time he came in I was hitting him back, *Bang, bang. Bang, bang* . . . by then I knew I could beat him but I wanted to make it look good for him at this point, I didn't wanna slag him off too much.

'Suddenly I thought, now I will take it seriously. I thought, I've boxed all my life so that's what I'll do. I'll treat it like a boxing match. I'll out-brain him. Remember, boxing's different from fighting. If you're tough, you don't give in, and most importantly if you've got a good brain for boxing you'll beat anybody. So from now on, every time he came in I hit him perfectly. I'd let him throw his jab, I'd dodge it and then I'd go *bang – bang*, just two punches every time. And every time I was hitting him I could feel the bones in me hand smashing. They were literally smashing. I couldn't let on, though. Sometimes I'd throw a punch and he'd duck and I'd hit the top of his head and you can imagine what that does to your hands. You've got nothing on them, you see? You really can feel the bones breaking. If you look at my hands now, they're smashed to pieces. I've got no knuckles. I had weak hands when I was a boxer as well. I used to have to wear a lot of bandages. Every fight I had as a pro I broke a bone in my hand somewhere along the line. Anyway, I keep hitting this guy every time he came in. And then he'd hit me back, in the ribs. At one point they stopped the fight 'cos his eye was cut. And from then on I thought, yeah – every time I went for him I knew exactly where I was going to hit him. I hit him on that eye, every single time. I'd line him up for a jab and I hit him exactly there, just rip him open. And it split more and more and still he kept on and on.

'Anyway, he kept on and on, he didn't know when to give in. They stopped the fight again and they flung a bucket of water over him, because he was all red with blood. I was red as well by now 'cos of my busted nose and mouth – but that was the only really good shot he caught me with. He got me in the ribs a few times but I was too clever for him. It was my boxing experience that helped me really, everything my dad taught me when I was little. It was all down to him. But my dad didn't like me fighting out in the field, he always liked me boxing in the ring, where you're meant to box, where you're meant to do things right – and of course that's what I'd have wanted to do, but unfortunately I'd been forced into this fight through other people. Perhaps it was my fault really, since I'd been gambling again. If I hadn't gone gambling I'd have not seen Bimi again.

'Still he kept on fighting. Every time I hit him, every time I'd break something else in my hand. Anyway next thing I know there's about 800 people gathered around us. And I knew this fight wasn't just due to go on for another five minutes, it was going to go on and on. You could see them coming from the stands, heading down towards us. All the travellers were with us by this point and things were getting really packed. People are sitting on top of caravans, cars and lorries – they're all over the place and they're shouting and screaming. It was scary, really. You didn't know whether you were gonna lean backwards and suddenly get a knife in your back or whatever. By now I was getting sick of the fight. I kept hitting him and still he kept on at me. He was a man who just didn't wanna pack in. But I suppose that's what it's all about – the last man standing walks away. Anyway, he just kept on and on and on.

'At one point there was a man nearby selling a horse for £3,000. It was on a chain, and the crowd were all coming over towards us, rushing and hollering, and the horse just bolted, scared. But it didn't stop running even though it had a chain around its neck. It broke its neck on the chain.

'And still the fight carried on. I kept hitting him and he kept splitting open. It got to a stage where it was horrifying to look at. I was beginning to get scared of hitting him because of the damage, even though he was the hardest man I'd fought. We just had to fight until some idiot decided to try and stop it.

'Suddenly Bimi's wife jumped in, 'cos by this time his eye was hanging down out of its socket, on his cheek. You can imagine how much blood was coming out. It really wasn't very nice and I ain't really that kind of fighter, but I didn't wanna back down – I had to do it. Anyway, his wife jumped in and said "Bimi, Bimi stop! Your eye's hanging out." And Bimi's angry at his wife and he smacked her. "Get out of the way, woman," he said. "I've got another eye." That was all he said! "Your eye's gone, your eye's gone," she was screaming. But *boom*, he was straight back at it again. Eventually a fella called Docherty jumped in and stopped it. By this time neither of us was giving their best. In the end no one won the fight. That's how it finished. But really, he was too small for me. He couldn't really handle my weight. If I hadn't known how to fight he'd have beaten me; he'd beaten most men he'd taken on already around that time. But I could fight, and I had a brain as well – I was just too tough for him at the time for him to beat me.

'At these fights, there's no doctor or referee, there's a best man. You pick the man who you think has got the most respect at that time from the men who are fighting. You pick a man who can fight, who's well respected, but who is a man who won't join in. And the other fighter does the same. Obviously this man can't join in 'cos it's up to him to watch out that there's fair play and sort any problems out. But what I'm talking about is really the old days. Nowadays it's all different. Back then people used to fight fair. They don't now. Nowadays you get people gassing each other, stabbing each other and cutting each other's throats. In the old days you'd have one man watching out for fair play, then your opponent would have some men with him and you'd have some men with you. Everyone would make a circle. If you didn't want a circle you'd go into a field. You'd take your shirt off, put your hands up and start. There'd be no kicking, no biting, no head-butting – just fists. You'd hit him anywhere you wanted to, but if a man goes down you wouldn't kick him in the mouth or stamp on his head. You wouldn't do any of that. When it was reaching the end, you'd go, "You had enough?" and he'd say "Yeah," and the fight would be over. And that's how it was. There were no real refs – just someone to watch and stop the fight when one of you has had enough. But if you are having a fair fight and you go down on the floor and your opponent kicks you, then your friends and family are entitled to give your opponent a kicking. Your best man is entitled to complain, too, and when that happens it causes riots.

'If you've got sensible people and you organise it properly, the old gypsy way, you'll have it under control, it will all go fine. Nowadays you just can't control it all. If you're fighting fair you're not allowed to kick a man when he's on the floor. The best man will grab you and say, "Oi – fucking well don't do things like that, or I'll hit you myself." Half the time the best man will probably be as good a fighter as the man who's fighting, or maybe better. This kind of fight was a big event in the gypsy calendar. They'd be looked forward to, talked about and bet upon. They'd be saying, "So-and-so's fighting so-and-so at the fair in three months' time. It's gonna be the best fight you ever did see!" There'd be gang-loads of travellers going. They'd come from the north, the south – even Scotland. That's how it used to be, that's what it was like in the old days. They'd all come on their horses and carts, it'd take some of them a week to get there but they'd get there. And it would be 100 per cent fair. People wouldn't be joining in with bats and things like that like they do nowadays.'

Bobby is a warm, friendly family man and good businessman. Nowadays he refuses to use his considerable fighting talent for anything other than defending his family or helping others who can't look after themselves. But if you meet him, don't let his charming manner fool you into thinking he is not as hard as nails. He still is. If you are a bully or you threaten his family you must be prepared to pay a terrible cost. For Bobby there are no grey areas – there is wrong and there is right. He would do or say anything to get out of fighting unless he thought you were deeply in the wrong. And once he has decided that there is no turning back, he will keep coming at you with a terrible force.

I left Bobby at his friend's gym to go in search of someone who could round the whole investigation up for me; someone who could tell me more about the violence and the respect involved in the scene, and about the men's need to fight and to watch fights. I contacted Dave Courtney.

FIFTEEN

DAVE COURTNEY HAD LIVED THE FIGHTING LIFE AND COME OUT the other side a changed man. He could look back and tell you why fighting is part of us, why we are fascinated by it and why some men are good at it.

Dave was the man who arranged Reggie Kray's funeral, and that rocketed him into the public eye. He was the subject of an award-winning BBC documentary called *The Bermondsey Boy* that showed him debt-collecting, throwing bad tenants out of their rich landlords' flats and meeting and greeting London's hardest characters like the late, great bare-knuckle fighter and unlicensed boxer Lenny McLean. They called Dave 'the yellow pages of crime' and so it was natural that I turned to him for help to find some answers. I was nervous about calling him. Why should he help me? What was he really like? Was he dangerous? What might he want in return?

'Come round the house,' he said. 'I'll give you an interview about fighting, not a problem.' When he gave me the address I immediately thought he was winding me up, but I didn't like to say so.

'Camelot Castle? Can you spell that for me please, Dave?'

'C–A–M–E–L–O–T. When you comin'?' he said.

In the car, crossing the Thames on the Woolwich Ferry, I wondered if I was doing the right thing going to see him at home. His photograph, which lay on the passenger seat next to me, showed Dave smoking a fat cigar, his shaven head and tanned face staring out at me. He was wearing a spangly jacket over a black shirt, white tie and waistcoat. Obviously not a shy man. I drove my way around the back streets of south London, got completely lost and eventually stopped to ask for directions.

'Excuse me – can you tell me how to get to Camelot Castle?'

'No idea, mate,' the man said, and he walked off shaking his head.

I looked across the road and saw a large white house at the end of the terrace. There was a huge painting covering one whole side wall. It had Dave Courtney astride a black stallion with his wife Jenny on the back. He was holding a sword up high. He was wearing a black shirt and trousers, like he was in the photograph. In the front garden on the patio, there was another sword, this time stuck in a white triangular stone.

The walls were indeed shaped like castle walls. Jenny let me in and made me a cup of coffee. When Dave came downstairs I began by asking him about his background.

'I was very naughty when I was young. I was your typical nightmare next-door neighbour's kid. I was the one that the other parents would say, "Don't go and play with him," about. I was that kid.

'I very much wanted to be older and out earning money from a very early age, which meant I had a lot of older friends. I'm not saying you turn into more of a coward when you get older but you're definitely braver as a child about doing things. You're just incredibly brave in whatever you take on as a child. And I was sort of used a bit, most probably, by the older people who whipped up that maverick spirit. "I'll do it, I'll get in there, I'll go first, I'll start it," – you know? I was one of those, kind of eager to please. But eager to please the wrong people, possibly. Now if I'd have been more eager to please at school or at home, maybe I wouldn't be sitting here today. But instead I was eager to please with the big bad boys and I sort of embarked on a life of petty crime at first and then it sort of grew into very major,

Premier Division stuff. I was a late starter when it came to the actual fighting in my life. You know I didn't realise I actually had a gift for it until later on, when I was 15 or 16. It wasn't like I was fighting at school all the time or anything like that. I found it a lot easier to be the court jester and get on with everybody and make everyone laugh rather than try to be the best fighter. I've never claimed to be the very best fighter. There are some stunningly good fighters out there. I'm very good, but I'm not the best by a long shot.

'Any genuine hard man will tell you that there's an awful lot of people out there who pretend to be hard, but they'll also tell you that once you have that inner confidence that you can actually really do it a lot better than most other people, there is no need to go around advertising the fact.'

I notice another picture – a three-foot-high oil painting of Dave, in a black shirt and trousers smoking the obligatory cigar. He continued, 'I was going boxing and all that at the time. I was being trained at the Fisher Club. The hierarchy of the criminal world are attracted to boxing for some reason. It actually attracts the naughty people. I think it's the love of blood sport in them. It's always been that way and it will always be that way. If one of your skills in life is fighting, some naughty man will recruit you somewhere to fit you into his little arsenal of weapons that he needs to do whatever he does in his life. He will recruit hard men and a lot of hard men have been through the boxing ranks, you know? I am one of them.

'I yearned for it. I saw that the boxing was like an apprenticeship for me to get into that little world, you know? I thought if I could actually be seen as an asset to these people in some way, then I would be recruited into their ranks by somebody. I saw that very early on and set out to make my mark in whatever field that it took to be one of them. What I didn't realise at the time was that the sort of people that I was looking at, the sort of people I wanted to be, were actually ex-gangsters. I didn't realise that until I actually *became* one of those people. They were people that had done it all and had now finished. But I didn't realise. I thought they were still gangsters. I thought I wanted to be a villain, but what I really wanted to be was an ex-gangster. You can't actually go around as flamboyant as a lot of these people are when you're still actually doing it all. You can only actually do the "get a load of me" bit when you've retired. But I didn't know that at such an early age so I ended up being a villain and still going, "Get a load of me," while I was at it, like an idiot, you know?'

Dave laughed and I presumed that I could as well. Slowly I began to realise that he was a born communicator.

'So I was caught. I shouldn't have driven about in flash cars, but I did. And that rubbed a few people up the wrong way. Well, I have my critics – an awful lot of them in the police force and some on my side of the fence as well.'

Dave's mobile phone rang somewhere in the background – *The Godfather* theme tune. Jenny came in with it. Dave chatted for a bit and then returned to our conversation. 'Yeah, I've got my critics and that is why, while I was still young, I decided to retire from the crime game – because I realised that what I actually wanted to be was an ex-criminal. The reason you chose to be a baddie is because you know you'll be bigger, newer, nicer, better than you would be on a five-day-week job flipping burgers in McDonalds. You know you ain't going to get the things you want doing that. Perhaps you achieve the financial position to get the things that you want, but then someone says to you, "Well you can't have the gold Rolex. You'd better not let her buy the white fox fur. You can't drive round in a Rolls Royce; try and buy a nice little low-key Mondeo." Well if I wanted to drive a Mondeo I would have carried on and flipped burgers in McDonalds, wouldn't I? I wanted all the good things, I didn't want to hide away and not be seen. So the best thing for me to do was to retire and live the glorified life. I'm not, for one second, saying please be a criminal. And I'm not glorifying crime. I'm glorifying Dave Courtney! I'd have been a glamorous postman. I'd have been a cocky butcher. I'd have been a flash bricklayer. I'm glorifying Dave Courtney, I'm not glorifying crime at all – although to the outside world I might make it look like a career option.

'I drive around in the Rolls Royce sometimes, but inside this place I ain't got a pint of milk in the fridge. You always look prosperous as a naughty man, as a villain. They always imagine you have thousands and all that but I just don't pay to go into nightclubs. I don't buy a drink when I'm in there either. The fact that I'm going out every night might mean that everyone assumes I'm a multimillionaire, but that's not necessarily the case, you know?

'My friends that I had then are still the same as I have now, they haven't changed. I don't get rid of true friends. In whatever walk of life I choose to go down as I get older, I am very well known for dragging my people with me – which is why the police find it very, very hard to swallow that I've retired, because I still have an array of very colourful, active friends and today you are guilty by association. I'm not prepared to actually ignore people that have defended me and helped me and have gone to prison for me and have got holes in their body down to me. The fact that I've now decided to turn my back on that way of life and get into another one doesn't mean I can turn my back on those people if they actually make it to my door for help and go, "Dave, I've just done something, I need somewhere to hide." I cannot go, "I'm sorry, I'm not in that life no more, go away." I'd have to tell them to come in and send them off to a disused caravan site in out-of-season Sheerness to stay there for six months or something, you know? I could not tell them I was no longer going to help them. The only possible way I could ever not help people is if I wasn't actually there to ask. I am the type that will go, "Yes, okay."

'In my younger days I aspired to be like Roy Shaw, Lenny McLean, Freddie Foreman, Joey Pyle, Tony Lambreano – all of them. I looked at them unashamedly, in awe. If you want to be like somebody, you have to be in their company to learn from them. I'm afraid a lot of this I learnt when I was in prison – but any given day I was in prison, if you asked me if I wanted to come home, I would have said, yes. Anyway, now I've done it and I've learnt things from being there. Those are a couple of years in my life that I would never change. That is the reason that older men say you should have national service and all that. They don't want the youth of today to go off to war but they want them to have one year out of their life, locked away from all their privileges, just to be with men. You learn about men and life and what your priorities are doing. When you go to prison your priorities get straightened out. You know who is more important – your wife, your girlfriend or your mates down the pub. You're in mental turmoil when you're out here – not knowing who you'll please and who you won't. But when you're in prison all your priorities come straight. You have one visit a month. Who do you want to see? You know who is still sending you letters after you've been there six months. You learn an awful lot, and I was lucky enough to learn an awful lot while I was there. I made a good name for myself while I was in there too. I came out and I surrounded myself with the people that I was in awe of as a young man.

'Everybody in the world makes their personality out of things that they nick from other people. We all do the same. You nick a bit of this or you'll hear someone with a little saying and you'll incorporate that into your vocabulary. I built Dave Courtney on what I thought all these people were about – respect, bravery, loyalty, morals. And if you do something long enough, you become it. If you go to a mental home for three years and you're straight when you go in there, by the time they let you out you're a nutter, you know? If you want to be a good footballer, you hang around with footballers. If you want to be a raver, you hang around with ravers. I have been lucky enough to have close friends and most of them are actual legends in the criminal world.

'The general public image of prison is that you go in and you come out cleverer; you've learnt all these new crimes in there. Well, that's not actually what happens. What actually happens is, you're locked away in a building for a year with a thousand people who done it wrong. You learn one thousand things *not* to do, one thousand things *not* to say in court and one thousand things *not* to do when you do this job. And it is drummed into you solidly, 24 hours a day for each year because all they talk about is, "Oh I done this, I done that." And if you get moved to another prison you learn another thousand things not to do. So when you're actually let out, you are two thousand things in your head better off than you were when you went in. So that's what happens. You haven't actually learnt to do anything different or new. You've just learnt how not to do it. So you become very good at it because you've learnt all the ways that you can get caught. That's how I learnt how not to go to prison; how not to do it.'

Dave began explaining how violence played a big part in his life. He told me, 'Fighting was an essential part of prison life. Prison was an awful lot more violent a long time ago than it is today. The racial problems were an awful lot more upfront than they are today. And fighting was a big part of it, yeah. When those heroes of mine were in prison, they were violent, I'm afraid. I mustn't say that, most probably they'll give me a slap round the earhole for saying it. But they were notoriously hard. You know they terrorised the place. People like Roy Shaw and Frankie Frasier terrorised the prison system with their willingness to jump up and fight anybody, anywhere, any time. Although they are perceived by some people as nutters, the Charles Bronsons of this world are actually quite talented, skilled men in the art of fear. Personally I think you've got to have grey areas in your life. Everything cannot be black and white, you have to bend a little bit. Well these people were 'non-benders'. It was just black and white for them. Screws and prisoners – you don't like us and we don't like you. That brought them an awful lot of trouble, which eventually gave them an awful lot of years. I should imagine a lot of them could have got out an awful lot quicker if they'd have just shut their mouths sometimes but they couldn't and they still can't today. I mean, Roy Shaw is 60 today and I don't know many men who would like a roll about the floor with Roy today at all – me being one of them.

'Roy Shaw and Lenny McLean were the people that actually gave me dreams of maybe being a professional boxer or something like that, you know? But anything I do, I like to think I'm at least very, very, very good at it – or the best at it. If I'm not, I won't do it. And once I actually saw the Roy Shaws and Lenny McLeans doing their bit in the boxing ring, I knew immediately that I was never ever going to be the best at that. To me anyway, they are wolves in sheep's clothing. Outside, to me they were just lovely, good people that I could really relate to and see where they were coming from. But in the ring they turned into these beasts from hell, you know? They just seemed impossible to hurt. It just seemed too hard to even bother fighting them because there was nothing in me that would beat that – especially when they're in full flow and they're bleeding and there's three thousand people screaming out your first name you know. It was "*Lenny! Lenny!*" You could have hit him on the head with a sledgehammer and he isn't going to go down.

'That's how you feel in there, trying to knock somebody out. And that is what is addictive about the fight game. That is why you get people like Sugar Ray Leonard and Larry Holmes and all that. They have comebacks not because they genuinely believe that they are as good as they used to be – but because they just miss that feeling so much. Even if you go out there and lose, to go out there man against man – it's the most natural combat, you know? It's a test for you. It's an awful lot of things to an awful lot of different people.

'Why do we want to watch it? Well it's exactly the same question if you went back and asked the Romans why they wanted to watch all those Christians being thrown in there with the lions. There's a little dark bit in the back of our minds that makes us like to watch and like to know. Even the people that outwardly say, "Well, I'm not interested, I think it's barbaric" – they've all read the books and watched the films and it's not something that will change in us. We are inquisitive about it because the majority of the general public haven't got that little bit of red mist that goes over them that makes them growl and scream like animals. They really need to know about people that are like that.

'I was on a bill with Lenny McLean once where I battered this guy and we was both standing up at the end, but because he had sold more tickets than me, they gave him the fight. And I just lost me rag and as all the corner-men were getting out of the ring, I grabbed the stool and boshed him round the earhole with it. I put him on the floor, out of it. Then everyone climbed into the ring and there was a big mass punch-up. Well that actually did it for me. That was the best fight I'd ever had. It was the most memorable thing I'd ever done in the ring. That actually helped me sell more tickets, you know what I mean? But I just was nowhere near as ferocious or big enough to actually put myself in their league. I might have been the best in my own weight, but these were heavyweights. These were big men. You get a 20st aggressive man literally running across the ring towards you and you're, like, *bang*. What you're taught to do is not going to stop that. You would hit him on the chin and then you would just go back to the ropes and he would grab you and start biting your ear off. You understand? No one can teach you to be like that. You've got to be born that way. You cannot learn to be powerfully vindictive, aggressive, animalistic and feel no pain. You can't learn that. You can learn the skills of boxing and the ducking and diving and the weaving and the Queensbury rules but no one can teach you to have that killer instinct. You are born with that. That is why I'm a firm believer that all that's in your genes. You're born naughty. You're born aggressive. You are born a slut or you are born frigid. You don't become these things. A proper hard man, a docker or something like that, when he's 25 is the same man when he's 80. He still thinks he can jump up and give you a smack in the chops if you're rude. It's just in him. He will still go, "Come on, you bastard I'll club you" – even if he hasn't got the capability to do it any more. These people like Roy Shaw and Lenny McLean had it in them. I wasn't of that calibre. So I decided to back out and be a fan rather than stay in and be a participant. I'm still a fan today. I love unlicensed boxing and have put on an awful lot of unlicensed shows with Joey Pyle. I've even helped his son, young Joey, now that he's in the professional game. But the most fun is when you're doing something that is perceived to be illegal and being in a building where something is happening where the police could kick the door down and run in and arrest everybody at any moment – it is exciting being there. The fights are an awful lot more exciting than they are in the professional ranks, too. You know you could go and pay five hundred quid for a ringside seat to go and watch Frank Bruno chin someone in the first round and the bloke says, "Yeah I'm still all right," and the ref goes, "No, no, no." And that's it! And you've paid five hundred quid for three minutes, you feel robbed. At least in the unlicensed game you know that someone is beat when he is lying on the floor bleeding out of every orifice. You know that it was a proper decision if it's stopped. You never feel cheated. The actual excitement of being somewhere that is illegal, even though you are not doing anything illegal yourself – that feeling that something's not supposed to be happening . . .

'Head-butting is not actually encouraged in these fights of ours, but you don't actually get penalised for it. You understand that but by the time some of these fighters realise how far the other person is prepared to go, it's too late, they've lost. You get an awful lot of fighters who have been professional boxers, but they got a little bit too old for the game and so they enter the unlicensed game. And their way of thinking is, well, because I'm an awful lot fitter and I have an awful lot more skills than this person I'm fighting here – he's nothing more than a football hooligan, or a tasty doorman, or just a hard-nut or whatever. He'll think, my skills and my technique will prolong the fight; will eventually help me to win it. That is how they would think. But the people that they'll be fighting will have been in the unlicensed game for a long time and they've picked up new rules – a new set of rules that ain't written down anywhere, and they're definitely not Queensbury rules you know?'

Dave stopped to light a large Churchill cigar, with great ceremony. He rolled it, smelled it, cut the end off with a knife and began to burn it. He put it in his mouth and puffed as he lit it. The aromatic smoke filled the room. We walked outside the house. I asked Dave one more question – the one I'd asked everyone: why do people feel compelled to watch two men fighting?

'We're all men – we've all got testosterone in our bodies. The feeling you get when there's a man lying on the floor unconscious and you're standing on top of him and everyone's shouting out your first name – it is almost a sexual experience. You could almost come.'

I said goodbye to Dave and Jenny and their baby Courtney and headed back to the office on the Isle of Dogs. Something else that Dave had said stuck in my mind.

'If you like ordinary boxing then you'll really like unlicensed boxing. If you like unlicensed boxing you'll really, really like bare-knuckle boxing. And after that, if there were two people still doing live gunfights at the OK Corral then we'd pay to go and watch that.'

He was absolutely right, we would.

If there is something I have learned from all of this and from the fighters I have met it is this: you don't have to use your fists to be tough. The definition of bravery is facing your darkest fears.

There's an old saying: it's not the size of the dog in a fight that counts, it's the size of the fight in a dog.

Roy Shaw told me: 'There's weak men and there's strong men. Strong men are different to other people. If we've got to fight, we do, and if it's to the death then so be it. If a bloke knifes you, well then – you knife him. You've got to end up the winner come what may.'

EPILOGUE

SO WHAT DID I LEARN FROM WRITING THIS BOOK AND PRODUCING two documentaries on these types of fighting? Partly it was simply that we are fascinated by violence and the participants in it. There's something in us that is both repelled by it and attracted to it at the same time. We want to touch and feel it, like the moth that thinks it can live inside the flame. Some of us make a conscious decision to watch fights – whether they be on television, or if they are live events open to the general public, or in hidden, underground events. But there is a more primal, everyday instinct too. If there was a fight on the street I defy anyone not to look at it. We choose to watch sporting events but we also can't help watching spontaneous acts of violence. Passing a car wreck on the roadside – we have to look. Seeing the ambulances there and the medics working and firemen cutting away debris doesn't put us off; it has the opposite effect: it increases our curiosity. Even though the wreckage may have been moved to the side of the road and does not obstruct us, we slow down to get a good look. Even though part of us is frightened about the carnage we might see, we still look. We can't help it; it's human nature. It's the same morbid fascination that compels us to watch fights. It's in all of us, from every walk of life and every social group.

For those of us who can't fight and won't fight, we still love to be able to boast that we have *seen* fights, especially ones that are on the edge of the law or – better still – blatantly breaking it. If we can actually say that we know the fighters themselves, some of the fascination that people have for them rubs off on us – this is what I call the 'I may not be hard but I know a man who is' syndrome. I found this to be true in my case. At a television conference I was introduced as 'the patron saint of unlicensed boxing'. People who had ignored me before suddenly looked at me in a different light. Some actually stepped back, mouths open, looking me up and down in amazement. You could tell what they were thinking: 'You wouldn't think it to look at him!' Women were particularly attentive. So for a while, whenever I met people who were interested, I embroidered my stories about the characters I had filmed and my technique improved with every telling. I produced tales of the fighters and displayed them for others to marvel at. I exaggerated the danger and perfected the jokes. In one conversation I remember saying 'I wasn't worried about taking a clump round the ear, but I didn't want to get knifed or shot.' This I meant, but it went down a storm and from then on I kept it in. It became a well-polished party piece that was more about me than getting to any truth about the fighters or their lives.

That's why in this book I have tried to keep my mouth shut and leave it up to the fighters and the promoters to tell their own stories in their own words. The glimpse of these fighters' lives and their characters that this book provides deserves a health warning: Do not get carried away by the image of the hard-talking men in this book; do not imagine that you can do the same things they have done. If you want to replicate their lives as street fighters and become 'hard men' there will be a price to pay. A friend of mine, Norman Parker, who I first met at the end of filming party that I held in Soho for everyone who appeared in the *Natural Born Fighters* documentary, paid that price. His life was wasted – 24 years of it was spent in prison. He was a wild, free spirit who escaped from a maximum security prison and was then recaptured. He had fights of such naked, free aggression that they earned him a gigantic reputation and yet more years on his jail sentence. But the physical and mental torment that he suffered would have split a weaker spirit in half. He survived. He has written a series of books called *Parkhurst Tales* in which he describes what it was like for him, a category-A prisoner, when he had to fight in prison – it is a terrifying nightmare. Facing an adversary armed with razors or a home-made knife, with only the one thought in his mind – either to win or die – takes a type of courage or self-destructiveness that few of us have.

Alan Mortlock spoke to me of many battles in which his own well-being did not seem to matter – and in which the damage that he could inflict on others was limitless. For Norman, Alan and many more, fighting was as much about taking punishment as it was about giving it. Roy Shaw saw it as a simple choice. He told me: 'There are weak men and there are strong men, and if strong men have to fight we do – and if it's to the death then so be it.' Dave Courtney sees it simply as a case of 'kill or be killed'. But it is more complex than that. I met men who were bullies, picking on men weaker than themselves and these men I despised and hated. I also met men who were bullied themselves. Ian 'The Machine' Freeman had been bullied and beaten so badly that he had thought of committing suicide. Yet he fought his own dark thoughts and became a lethal street fighter and skilled ultimate fighter. I met men whose emotions were extreme; men who were capable of great loyalty and friendship and compassion one minute and could snap into extreme, uncontrolled violence the next. Lawrence Hiller, a good friend of mine who helped me find most of the contacts for my documentary, was once driving an ex-doorman to my office for an interview. On the drive coming east on the A406, a boy racer cut in front of the car and shouted abuse at Lawrence. At the red lights the ex-doorman jumped out of the car, incensed by the liberty that had been taken and keen to seek justice. On that occasion the petrified driver was lucky to escape the beating of his life. And if he had been beaten up, there is a part of me that would have applauded the deed. I would have liked to have done the same thing myself but I know I could not. The men in this book are anti-heroes. They are rebels. They do things that we wish we could do. In a strange way, we need them – we need their strength. It makes us feel less weak.